The Commitment Chronicles

THE POWER OF STAYING TOGETHER

Cheryl McClary

SOURCEBOOKS, INC.
NAPERVILLE, ILLINOIS

Published by Sourcebooks, Inc.
P.O. Box 4410, Naperville, Illinois   60567-4410
(630) 961-3900
Fax: (630) 961-2168
www.sourcebooks.com

Library of Congress Cataloging-in-Publication Data
McClary, Cheryl.
  The commitment chronicles: the power of staying together/Cheryl McClary.
      p.cm.
Includes bibliographical references.
ISBN-13: 978-1-4022-0648-1
ISBN-10: 1-4022-0648-8
1. Marriage. 2. Man-woman relationships. 3. Commitment (Psychology). 4. Married
people–Psychology. 5. Married women–Psychology. I. Title.
HQ734.M44236 2006
646.7'8–dc22
              2005025016

Printed and bound in the United States of America.
DR   10   9   8   7   6   5   4   3   2   1

In memory of Susan Elizabeth McClary:
my sister, guardian angel, and soul mate.
You are always with me.

To Jim:
Thank you, Handsome Man.
I love you forever.

To Clint and Wyatt:
I treasure you each and every moment of my life.

To Mom, Dad, and my beautiful sisters:
Thank you for having the love and courage to love me
for who I was, who I was becoming, and who I am. I
am so blessed to have you as my family.

Contents

Acknowledgments vii

What Is Real Love? ix

Preface: Why I Wrote This Book xi

Introduction: Amazing Grace xv

SECTION I: Are You Really or Surreally in Love?

1. The Premarital Foreplay of Surreal Love 3

2. Any Woman Can O.D. on Surreal Love 19

3. Regaining Consciousness 43

SECTION II: Take Charge to Love, Honor, and Cherish Thyself

4. The Price You Pay for Finding You Is—Love 63

5. Save Your Soul by Becoming Whole 69

6. Don't Worry—"Stressed" Is "Desserts"
   Spelled Backwards 101

SECTION III: The Outpatient Recovery Guide for Women

7. Learn From the Mistakes of Others—You Can't Make Them
   All Yourself 113

8. A Simple Guide to Emotional Healing 121

9. It Takes Strength to Love. It Takes Courage
   to Be Loved 145

SECTION IV: How to Recognize and Treat R.A.D.S.
(Relationship Attention Deficit Syndrome)

10. Connecting with the Clueless Male 161
11. Teaching Him to Cut the Crap 183
12. Enabling Him to Make Love Longer Than He
    Can Go Shopping 205
13. Taking Him to the Limit One More Time 231
14. One Day at a Time, Sweet Jesus 245

Bibliography 259
Resources 261

Acknowledgments

It takes a village to raise a book. My village leader is Michael Hester. You helped me find and restore my faith in life and love. What a gift you are to me and to everyone whose life you have touched.

My village was filled with some of the best writers and editors in the business. Alison Fields rescued my manuscript and me every time I felt like giving up. She carried me back to the hut and gave me the expertise I needed to keep writing.

I adore my students. You are a continuing source of strength and inspiration. I love my time with you.

Marilou Awiakta, Victoria Pryor, Tony Rollman, and Susan Reinhardt—thank you from the bottom of my heart. You believed in me and gave me the courage to keep writing.

Special thanks to Shirley Geter and Amy Edwards, who provided the technical support for my entire village. Your skills blow me away. Someday I'll move to Mayberry where I belong. You both deserve the Medal of Honor for your skill, fortitude, endless patience, and dear friendship.

Ellen Boyd, Janice Coverdale, and Evelyn Lyles—God smiled on me when you became part of my life. We are destined to be together forever.

Trip Huxley, you amaze me with your creativity. It lights my soul every time I see your work.

To all my friends at the Army War College—you gave me the experience of a lifetime and my village ain't been the same since. I will never forget you. "Go Pikers!"

Karen Tessier of Market Connections—besides being brilliant and the best publicist anyone could ever ask for, you are also my most special friend and I treasure you. I thank God for sending you to be my guardian. You are wild, wonderful, and I love you from the bottom of my heart.

And Marla Cilley—what a beautiful Godbreeze I received when you became my cherished friend.

Last, but not least, I wish to honor my agent, Jeff Herman. Not only are you a great man and joy to work with; you also personify a "perfect gentleman." Thank you for loving and believing in *The Commitment Chronicles*.

Cheryl McClary

What Is Real Love?

- **Real Love** is knowing how to recognize when you have fallen in love because of childhood or past relationship baggage.
- **Real Love** is recognizing that the very same things that irritate you now are probably the same things that made you fall in love with him in the first place.
- **Real Love** is accepting that crisis in marriage can be healthy and seen as an opportunity for growth.
- **Real Love** is living your life to experience joy, rather than trying to avoid pain.
- **Real Love** is understanding that marriage makes you married, but commitment is an act of will that must be renewed daily.
- **Real Love** is saying that it's okay to complain.
- **Real Love** is asking: "What would Real Love for myself do now?"

- **Real Love** is loving yourself enough to listen to what your body is trying to tell you.
- **Real Love** is being honest with yourself and having the respect to follow your own wisdom.
- **Real Love** is recognizing that you are responsible for your own healing, wholeness, and happiness.
- **Real Love** is realizing that your ability to create change is your greatest power.
- **Real Love** means loving him like you've never been hurt, dancing like nobody's watching, and living like there's no tomorrow.

~~~

Preface: Why I Wrote This Book

It was March 1, 2001, when I read Dear Abby's column in the paper. My heart broke as I read the desperate plea for help from "Tired of It All." I was all too familiar with the pain she was feeling. Not only had I been through it myself, but I hear her story nearly every day from woman after woman.

Abby is an expert and I usually agree with her responses. But this time, she missed the mark. I immediately fired off the following letter:

March 2, 2001

Dear Abby:

This letter is in response to the woman who wrote that she was "Tired of It All." As a women's health professor, I hear her life story from hundreds of women year after year. I'm convinced there are thousands of women in her same situation who are married to doctors, lawyers, accountants, etc., who seem to be nice guys at the office and in society, but at home they are obnoxious, clueless, and mostly unconscious when it comes to their relationships. You were right when you said leaving wasn't an option. I applaud you and her for encouraging commitment. Unless a relationship is abusive, divorce hurts everyone, particularly the children. There are no winners in a divorce.

The rest of your advice also was absolutely true, but it won't work. No amount of convincing, no matter how kind and loving, will make an impression on a man who doesn't believe he is depressed and is "happy" with his marriage. He thinks he is just FINE and all he wants is for her to leave him alone and be happy with the way things are.

It is crucial that the woman understands that she can change and control only one thing in her life: HERSELF. She should stop wasting her energy trying to change him. She should immediately quit concentrating on him and begin directing her energy towards finding and building her own self-wellness and emotional wholeness. I realize this is easier said than done, but it is a lot easier than having her soul suffocated on a daily basis by her husband.

As she focuses her attention on HERSELF and begins to find real love for HERSELF, the whole dynamic of her relationship will begin to change. Her growth will be her strength. She will be a leader instead of a follower in her marriage. This may not change him, but it will cause him to change his behavior. She will become strong enough, not only to get his attention and teach him to "cut the crap," but more importantly, she can begin living her life fully and with enthusiasm.

Sincerely,

Cheryl McClary, Ph.D., J.D.
Associate Professor
Department of Health Promotion
Univ. of North Carolina Asheville

P.S. If she will give me permission, I will be more than happy to send "Tired" all my lecture presentations on "Finding Self-Wellness," "Discovering Real Love in Your Relationship," and "How to Connect with a Clueless Partner."

As I signed the letter, I was shocked at how I was feeling. I was truly frightened that there might be no way for me to get information to "Tired of It All." I had two choices: I could continue to worry about her and all the other women suffering from the same type of dilemma, or I could try my best to put my notes and experience into a book that had the potential to reach all women who want commitment and love in their relationships. So here it is—*The Commitment Chronicles*. I wrote it for all of us who are "Tired of It All" and want love and happiness. We deserve it and we can have it. Here's how.

~

Introduction: Amazing Grace

I'm sitting at one of the finest, most exquisite restaurants in New Orleans. My husband made plane and dinner reservations for this wonderful evening months ago to surprise me for our twenty-third wedding anniversary. He orders us my all-time favorite drink—two top-shelf margaritas on the rocks with salt.

Jim is grinning from ear to ear. I'm not sure if it's because he's so proud of himself for actually remembering our anniversary this year, or if it is because he knows he's going to get plenty of "atta boys" tonight for this one. Our drinks come and he raises his glass to toast his "lovely wife and twenty-three years of marriage."

As I clink my glass to his, I am thinking—How in the hell have we stayed married this long? How have we kept the commitment? How have we kept from leaving each other, much less killing each other? I mean, really, whoever put "until death do us part" in the traditional marriage vows centuries ago had obviously never been married. Or maybe the average life span was so short back then it was no big deal to stay married until you croaked at age thirty. But now! With today's medical advances, my college students who get married "until death do us part" could be looking at close to a hundred years of marriage. We're talking commitment big time!

As I continued to stare at my handsome husband, I finally popped the question. I asked him how in the world had we managed to be together for so long and still be great friends and stay in love. His answer was immediate and simple—"Honey, I just followed your lead." Talk about out of the mouths of babes! This is one of the few times that I agreed with him on something 100 percent! He was absolutely right. I had made a husband and a partner out of my man. I brought out the loving humanity that was buried deep within his testosterone. I didn't change him, I found him. I was and always will be committed to us. We have kept our commitment to each other because even though my husband was clueless, he had the amazing grace to follow my lead.

I have written this book for you because students, clients, audiences, and friends have been begging me to for years. I wish someone had written this book for me twenty years ago. When I said "I do" at age twenty-five, I had no idea what to do to keep us from dumping each other once the honeymoon was over and he got a remote control! I figured out how to "take the lead" the hard way, through the school of desperation and hard knocks.

As I continued to sip my drink and enjoy the best barbecue shrimp in the world, I continued to look at my husband with a deep sense of puzzlement. With his usual outstanding verbal communication skills, he asked me, "Whassup?" I answered him by saying that I understood how we have remained committed, but that, in itself, begs the question: Why? Why is commitment worth all the effort that goes into making it work? Well, Jim rolled his eyes as if this was the dumbest question he'd ever heard and answered me without hesitation.

"Cheryl," he said, "it is human nature to commit to another. No one wants to be alone, particularly men. And the reason one should stay committed to the same person is threefold. First, men have a profound resistance to change. We really don't want to change partners. Secondly, just like the first answer you choose on a multiple-choice exam is nearly always the right one, your first choice in a wife is usually the right one. The grass is never greener on the other side. And last, but not least, men are basically lazy and cheapskates. They do not want to go to the expense, time, or effort to plant and grow a whole new damn lawn. In summary, commitment is stability—stability for the children, the family, and each other. I like that. Now can we get dessert?"

Well, kiss my grits! The irony of this entire conversation did not escape me, nor my slightly margarita-influenced brain. I mean, here I was, a product of Southern culture where being ladylike is revered by men even more than having a gun rack, and I was also a dues-paying member of the country music songwriters industry which seemed to be a culture within itself—a culture where low-life men are either trying to get even with, get away from, or avoid being at the receiving end of a "Bobbit" from some woman.

My entire dating and married life could be chronicled by the hooks of the country songs I had written over the past twenty-five years:

> **Dating**—"Send Me a Man"
>
> **Breakups**—"There Are Two Sides to Every Story, Darlin'—Your Side and the Truth"
>
> **Marriage**—"You Are All I Need to Make My Dreams Come True"
>
> **Sex**—"He Keeps Comin' on Like a Summer Storm"
>
> **Children**—"I'm True and Dedicated to a Place Decorated With Ferns, Plastic Grapes, and Kids"
>
> **His obsession with work**—"Kids Can't Understand Things That Grown-Ups Can; Daddy Please Come Back Home"
>
> **My disillusionment with my marriage**—"I Can Bring Back Happy Memories with Bourbon, with Coffee All I Do Is Cry"
>
> **My continued disillusionment with marriage**—"Having a Husband Is Much Harder Than Having a Baby"

And last but not least, my true appreciation for the incredible man sitting across from me, who had somehow condensed life's most intriguing questions about commitment to multiple choice answers, fear of change, and mowing a lawn—"He May Be Clueless but He's a Keeper."

I had to give the guy credit. As a women's health professor, attorney, woman, wife, and mother, I knew his common sense explanation was strongly supported by social science research. Commitment works. We live in a world of expected instant gratification: faxes, cell phones, sound bytes, email, computers, and TVs. Everything is changing so constantly and quickly that we can't get our bearings. In today's hectic world, we need stability more than ever in our personal lives. This is the gift of grace that staying committed can give us.

So here it is—your lead. I have chronicled my dating and married life for you, knowing that it will change your life as it has for thousands of students, clients, and friends.

What's in It for You?

You are probably wondering what this book will do for you. Well, I don't want to waste your time trying to impress you with all the politically correct self-help psychobabble that might be appropriate about now. Just like the rest of this book, I'm going to cut to the chase and say it simply and in plain English. The benefits you will get from this book are:

1. You will finally understand why, out of all the guys you have known, you fell for him.
2. You will learn why you love him, yet sometimes can barely stand him.
3. You will learn how to love him even when you can barely stand him.
4. You will become adept at putting the balance back in the "for better, for worse."

5. You will recognize your own clueless behavior toward your partner, and immediately know how to enact positive change.

6. You will find power in staying together yourself, even when you feel you are falling apart.

7. You will feel better than you feel right now because Real Love will change your life.

8. Even though he says he's listening, you will learn how to get his *attention*.

9. You can enable him to bond with you instead of with himself some of the time.

10. You can teach him how to be as nice to you as he is to everyone at the office.

11. You can help him to feel—an "F" word he has barely identified with before.

12. You will have more fun with your mate and put the giggles back in your relationship.

13. You will find out how to stop his pouting and/or being a brat.

14. You will put the "I do" back in your love life and find out all sorts of fun ways "to have and to hold."

15. You will learn how to stay together, even when you are in a relationship.

In summary, you will learn how to find and nourish *yourself* first, and then give a man the honor and privilege of being a part of your life.

Warning! Warning! Read This First:

Make absolutely sure you completely understand that the kind of husband I'm talking about can be emotionally clueless, difficult, and even kind of obnoxious. But this is not a man who is abusive. He is not abusive verbally, emotionally, or physically. Dealing with an abusive man requires tactics in addition to what this book discusses, so acknowledge abuse if it exists in your relationship. Typically, evidence of physical battering can be seen, felt, and heard. Evidence of emotional or verbal abuse can be more difficult to identify. So please pay attention. You are probably in an emotionally or verbally abusive relationship if he makes you feel like:

> You're such slime you just oozed under the door.
> He is stuck with you.
> You make his life miserable.
> No matter how hard you try, you never act or look good enough for him.
> You are not safe.
> You are being completely controlled.
> You can't ever be yourself or really relax around him.
> You are always wrong, crazy, or confused.
> You have been "attacked."
> You are powerless.
> You are worthless.
> You are invisible.

If you feel any one of these, the odds are that you are in a relationship that has been, is, or can be abusive. If you think there's any chance of this, keep reading this book because you need all the empowerment you can get. And immediately get additional help. See a counselor and start reading the books about abuse listed in the Resource Section of this book.

{SECTION I}

Are You Really or Surreally in Love?

1

The Premarital Foreplay of Surreal Love

COMMITMENT AND CONSCIOUSNESS MAKE STRANGE BEDFELLOWS

I would love to be able to say that my husband and I have a totally conscious marriage. It would give me great peace and joy to be able to tell you that I have revitalized our marriage of twenty-three years by opening up and healing our past wounds and baggage. How wonderful it would be to show you how we have built a spiritual connection of unparalleled growth and development. But I can't. If you knew us, you'd already be laughing at the thought of it.

We don't have any of that "soul mate" stuff (at least not in the Hollywood movie, "spiritual twin" conventional sense of the word). And, as a couple, we probably never will. I'm pretty sure

Jim was an armadillo in a previous life. He's made it to human form in this lifetime, but there's still enough armor around him to keep him unconscious for the duration. Revisiting his childhood is not an option. I've had enough trouble just getting him to stop behaving as if he is still in his childhood. Heaven forbid he should get any more time being an adolescent in emotional puberty.

So, what am I saying here? I'm simply saying I have found Real Love for my rather unconscious husband and I love that we are committed to each other. I like snuggling with a hairy Neanderthal before I go to sleep and when I wake up in the morning. I like having my man in my life. He's not even close to what talk shows, self-help books, and the media expect him to be. He's not my "divine soul mate," or "spiritual partner," or even my closest friend. He's simply my handsome man, my husband, one of my best friends, and in his own weird way, he's always there for me. I love him: always have and always will. And, as with nearly all men, you can't change them per se, but you sure can change you. And this will always change his behavior in the relationship. Please note that for simplicity's sake (and because I wrote this book, not my husband), I focused this book on clueless traits of men. However, we women can be just as guilty of downright obnoxious behavior in our relationships. But since we will be the ones to take the lead to change our behavior and his, I'll stick with using examples of men's cluelessness, knowing you will recognize yourself when the need arises.

So, the promise of this book is simple. With all the insight I have gained through keeping the best of what worked for us and tossing the rest, I want to help you find Real Love through healing and wholeness.

COMMITMENT HAS A NEW FACE

After staying committed to the same man through thick and thin, sickness and health, hell and high water, in-laws and outlaws, until death do us part, forever and forever (i.e., for a damn long time), I've concluded a few things. No longer do women just grin and bear it. The face of commitment has changed. The days are gone when a woman would put up with anything just to keep a man. Its new face requires that a woman be strong and independent. She must be happy within and for herself. She should be journeying towards wholeness. She must know and understand Real Love. And she has to know how to take the lead in her relationship.

One could argue that those are also the requirements needed for a woman to divorce. And they would be right. But unless it's an abusive relationship, why get a divorce if there is a real possibility you could make it work if you just knew how? The most common response I hear from women who have divorced and remarried is, "I'm back in the same situation—just a different set of problems with a different guy." And even though approximately twenty million Americans have been divorced, almost everyone who gets divorced eventually remarries. I think this means that most of us like being in a committed relationship. And nearly all social scientists back me up on the theory that changing partners to try and find a better relationship is not the answer. Trying to find "Mr. Right" is a fantasy. Dr. Sills, in her book, *A Fine Romance*, says that "love isn't something you find; it's something you develop." Love is less a matter of the person you choose than of the kind of relationship you are able to create.

Commitment is a win-win situation. Men can be such difficult creatures sometimes, but commitment is worth the effort. Commitment eases our feelings of anxiety and depression in an increasingly disconnected society. Children who have parents who are committed to each other have lower anxiety levels and fewer anxiety-linked physical ailments. Marriage guru Dr. John Gottman says that after children, men are the biggest beneficiaries of marriage. Married men live longer and have fewer infectious illnesses and heart attacks. They are better off psychologically and physically, regardless of the quality of the marriage. As for women, a good marriage benefits our health and longevity as well. This new paradigm of commitment is a glorious gift to you, your relationship, and to society.

If you're like me, unless there's a picture of chocolate or Nicolas Cage naked on the cover, there is no way I'll make it through a whole self-help book. So I'm going to cut to the chase, tell you my story, and present you with all the insight I've acquired through and after years of experiential, behavioral, spiritual, and academic learning (i.e., years of screwing up)!

SURREAL LOVE VS. REAL LOVE

Before I get started going back in time to my own dating fiascos, I need to point out that relationships are too individual and complex for anyone to think they could be an expert in them. However, I am an expert in women's health, which includes emotional health, which of course includes relationships. But

I'll tell you right up front: this book is not politically correct or socially proper. It is a streetwise, straight shootin', fun, real life book that will work for you. I am purposefully writing this book this way because I wish someone had written me a "kick ass" book twenty years ago that could have knocked me out of the marriage coma I was in.

When I married my husband I was sure it was the real thing, Real Love. It looked right, felt right, and fit right. We were so in love. Whenever he would go out of town, I would miss him so much, I would have to go through our house and turn all my framed pictures of him face down. If I had to go on a trip, he would go to sleep each night holding one of my sweaters until I returned. On Valentine's Day the newspaper even did a story about our special marriage. Sounds like the real thing, doesn't it?

But it wasn't.

You see, the kind of love we had for each other was the kind of love that most couples have. It is the kind of love that causes nearly half of all marriages to fail. It's also the kind of love that causes the deadness that I see in the eyes of so many couples that are still married. It suffocates your soul. I call it "Surreal Love." Surreal Love is love, but it is a dreamlike distortion of Real Love. Nearly all men are most comfortable with Surreal Love and nearly all women want Real Love, but don't know how to get it.

It took me a long time to figure out the difference between Surreal and Real Love. And not knowing this difference for so long almost cost me my marriage. Even more importantly, it almost cost me myself. I was seriously thinking of leaving Jim. But I wasn't sure why. Our relationship was not abusive; it just wasn't happy. Let me rephrase that: I wasn't happy. And so I thought maybe if I changed partners, I'd find happiness. But after I thought about it, I realized that my friends who were divorced and remarried weren't all that happy either.

The other problem was that Jim and I still loved each other. I just didn't like the way he was acting. It seemed as if he was great to everyone at work, social gatherings, etc.—but he could be such a jerk when he got home. Why hadn't I been wise enough to know that when he promised to "forsake all others" this did not include television or computers? To top off my confusion, he was happy. He really believed everything was fine. But it wasn't to me.

What had happened? Had I outgrown him? Had I gotten tired of being married? Was my life simply too hectic to work on my relationship? Or, was it probably a little of all these things? I didn't know and, by that point, I didn't care. All I knew was that it was time for a change and it was up to me to do it. It was no longer acceptable for either one of us to continue behaving the way we were. I had read that 75 percent of all marriages are ended by the wife. Well then, why couldn't wives be the ones to save the marriage and try to make it work for us?

I will never again lose sight of how much power I have in my own life and his. I will always be growing towards self-wellness and wholeness. Finding Real Love for me gives me absolute confidence that I can healthfully handle anything my marriage has to dish out at me. I truly don't spend one minute anymore wondering what's going to happen next in my relationship. It is one day at a time, and I enjoy as much of it as I can.

Three "C's" of Commitment

This new relationship I have with myself requires the "3 C's": a conscious, continual, confirming commitment on my part. I love spending my valuable time forging a new relationship with myself, rather than working on fixing him. This means creating, feeling, internalizing, and really living my life through an enthusiastic love of who I am. No matter how obnoxious my husband can get, I finally feel rich and full: full of wonder, power, and beauty. This fullness is self-wellness that is required for Real Love.

THE ARMADILLO THEORY

I wasn't kidding about my husband's armadillo past. There is scientific evidence to back me up on this. You see, for centuries men outlived women. Until the advent of the germ theory and antibiotics, childbirth kept bumping us off too early. We didn't start living longer than men until the 1900s. Because of this, I think women have been evolutionarily recycled much more frequently than men. We have lived so many lives that we are emotionally and spiritually light years ahead of men.

Finding Real Love is completely within our control. As women, we are the ones in the pilot seat. We are at the controls of our relationship and ourselves. We have the lead. We have the choice to let trying to stay committed keep making us distressed or learn how to turn the commitment between men and women into the most life-giving, beautiful gift of Real Love.

Young Woman Finds Love in the Twilight Zone of Surrealness

I am still amazed at how long it took me to know Real Love. The entire time I was dating and even into the early years of being married, I lived in the dreamlike, distorted image of love that I now know wasn't Real Love. It was "Surreal," fake, and for the short term, it felt absolutely like the real thing. But to make commitment last, you need Real Love.

For me to really understand why I wanted to leave my husband several years ago, I had to take the emotional journey back to when men first began becoming an important part of my life. I had to really look at what role my choices in dating relationships played in my developing sense of who I was or wasn't. Going back in the time machine to 1975, when I was in my twenties and finally getting asked out, would reveal more to me about what Real Love is or is not than I ever imagined possible.

Tarzan and Larry King are Wrong Reasons to Get Married!

I can see it so clearly now as I look back over all of my dating screw-ups throughout the years. Let me try to explain. I believe that there are basically four reasons we fall in Surreal Love. I'll call them my "theories." I have lived and loved through them all. They are "backed up" in a more scientific way by the widely read psychologist Dr. Harville Hendrix. But I had to explain and understand them in a much simpler way. I am pretty sure they will help you better understand how to make Real Love happen in your relationship. (Otherwise, believe me, there would be no way I would put myself through this embarrassment!)

"Me Tarzan—You Jane" Theory

Okay, I'll own up to it. Underneath my civilized veneer bubbles a pot of purely instinctual brew of primal origins that can cause me to fall madly and uncontrollably in love with men who are "beef," the "bomb," i.e., the Tarzans, Supermen, James Bonds, and CEOs of the world.

Instinct points me toward men who will enhance the survival of the family, i.e., the silver backed gorilla, the corporate president who lords and dominates over other men and certainly women. My survivalist nature seeks the guy with "alpha" qualities—the guy who will bring home not only the bacon, but more than his share of the kill. Whether he does this because of physical prowess or financial acumen is insignificant. This theory explains why I could go "gaga" for the rich, wrinkled old president of "Megabite Denture" Corp. as easily, if not more so, as I would for a young, gorgeous starving artist. Or, why I might fall in a dead faint in the proximity of the "Ultimate Warrior" wrestling champion and totally ignore the sweet, smart, absolutely adorable ringside cameraman.

My Tarzan was named Ken. I fell in love with Ken the moment I saw him. He was tall, strong, and handsome. The "Barbie" that was hanging on his arm was a former Miss Alabama. My date (or I should say my half-date because I was twice as tall as he was) informed me that Ken's daddy was one of the wealthiest men in the state. (Oh still my beating heart!) My Surreal Love for Ken was completely out of control. Even though my half-date was one of the world's nicest and smartest men, all I wanted to do was brush him off so I could better concentrate on staring at Ken. Surreal Love is deceiving. It can feel so strong that you ignore what is important in life. It seems so powerful that even if you've got braces and a pizza face like I did, you think if Ken would just notice you, that he would marry you and you'd be happy forever.

Wrong! But I was young and goofy and didn't know it at the time. Ken finally did notice me, however. But only because "Barbie" accidentally dropped her fondue fork and speared my foot. Ken and everyone else had a good laugh. Of course, Ken's laugh was the most adorable laugh I had ever heard. Did I mention he was gorgeous?

Larry King Live Theory

This could also be called the Donald Trump theory, but the thought of naming one more thing after him makes me gag. Trump Tower—really! A man with any class at all could have gone with D.T. Diner & Lodging. Anyway, I will stick with Larry King because I usually like his show.

Under this theory, I would fall in love by carrying the Tarzan concept to the extreme. I'm talking about falling for men who are "pure plutonium." These are radioactive guys who emit alpha particles at a constant rate twenty-four hours a day. Under this theory, I would be attracted to a man who would become my source of identity. The face I showed to other people was the mask of my boyfriend. And, the more famous the mask, the greater my projected image. Think Ivana Trump, Monica Lewinsky, whoever Larry King's new young wife is now—is this number six? This theory can also be active in smaller ponds where the big fish are the boss, the doctor, the professor— whomever the woman perceives as a mate whose superior status will raise her own. You know the type of relationship I'm talking about. And you also know they usually don't work. Why? Because there is not a heck of a chance I would have ever dated this type of guy if he had not been "famous."

"Famous" is defined in different ways by all of us, but no matter how you define it, it can be fleeting and false, and this is nothing on which to base true love. We all want to be proud of how our partner is perceived by others, but lasting love only occurs if we're also as proud not only of how others view *us* but also of how we view ourselves.

Well, back to my dating life. Actually, it would be more accurate to say non-dating life. I was 21 years old and hadn't even had a phone call from a guy in over six months. I was so desperate that I finally agreed to let a girl I worked with fix me up with a "blind date." He arrived at my place over forty-five minutes late. I begrudgingly open the door. It's Ken! At the same time I'm carrying on about what a small world it is, he's mumbling that he's never met me before. But it's Ken! My true love, my destiny! What do I care that I was previously unnoticeable to him?

Ken took me to a huge party being given by the governor. Everybody who was anybody was there. I was Ken's date! I was finally a somebody! My image of myself with him was so skewed that I was very proud of him for flirting with every woman at the party.

Ken asked me out ten more times over a five-year period. It still scares me to think that I almost had a PhD, but I would have dropped it all if Ken had ever asked me to. I was so in love with Ken's looks, money, and social status that I totally over-looked the fact that he only called me after one of his dates was a last minute no-show. But, boy howdy, he could always count on me. I would call in sick at work, miss class, cancel on my friends, whatever it took to be with Ken. Surreal Love is danger-ous. Not only because it is never the basis for a healthy, real rela-tionship, but more importantly, because it causes you to become someone you would never want to be. I don't like very much of anything I did for Ken, but I despise the fact that my self-image was so low that I was in dire need of his.

How did it all end? I wish I could say that by learning to value myself, I learned to see through and not need the Kens of the world. But that didn't come until much later.

On our eleventh date, Ken didn't take me to a fancy party, an expensive restaurant, or even to box seats at the football game. He took me to a friend's rather sleazy apartment to fill in for a game of penny poker. I was the big winner with $10.98. When I excused myself to go to the bathroom, Ken took my money. Turns out Ken's daddy had decided to quit supporting him. Just because Ken had turned 30, his mean old daddy wanted him to grow up and get a job. I was lucky. Ken's misfortune helped me to grow up and get a life. Without his money, fancy clothes, and fancy places, he wasn't my dream guy anymore. That's Surreal Love for you. It's as shallow as it makes you feel, and I was feeling pretty shallow. We had nothing in common except a desire for my $10.98. I turned Ken down the next time he called.

"He's Got a Great Personality!" Theory

This theory really depends on what you value in yourself. I valued things such as being athletic, having a love of travel, being smart or creative, you know—some of the few things I was aware enough to love about myself. I was proud of these qualities, so I searched for a man who also treasured these qualities in himself and me. Theoretically, if you have a good, strong, powerful sense of self-esteem, you will only be able to love someone with good self-esteem.

Unfortunately, the sad part of this theory is that it easily explains why so many women are "looking for love in all the wrong places." Like attracts like. Insecure women with low self-esteem always seem to fall for guys who are insecure and have low self-esteem.

As you've probably already guessed, my dating life was still continuing to circle the drain. I know it sounds like an oxymoron, but I finally met my "Mr. Personality" at a Young Republicans meeting. Everyone kept coming over to tell me that I would just "love him" because he had the best personality. Well, they were right. His self-deprecating sense of humor was as clever and funny as my own. He and I automatically were the center of any party. We could crack up everyone with our ability to be so funny at our own expense.

Everyone we knew thought Allen and Cheryl were perfect for each other. Because our lack of self-esteem was about the same, we were amazingly comfortable together. We never said an unkind word to each other; we never hurt each other's feelings; we never argued; and we always smiled. It felt so right. For over six months I was so in love with Allen. Then it happened. I learned that Surreal Love is dishonest. Allen and I would never tell each other the truth about ourselves, each other, or anything else because we were too afraid and too fragile to risk not being liked.

We fell out of love on a Friday night. It was the only Friday night we hadn't gone out with each other in six months. For some reason, I was tired and wanted to be alone. I didn't want to hurt Allen's feelings, so I lied. I told him I was sick and thought I might be getting typhoid fever! Allen couldn't even tell me that was the dumbest, most lame excuse he had ever heard. Instead, he sent me flowers and a get-well card.

Things between us were never the same after that night. We didn't understand how and why it happened; we only understood that something didn't feel right anymore. It's so easy to see now that two insecure people can only produce a surreal type of love. Also, I need to mention here what I mean by insecurity. On the surface, both Allen and I appeared to have our acts together. Allen was an extremely gifted microbiology graduate student whose research was already widely published in leading scientific journals. I was in graduate school on a full academic scholarship. Allen and I met at a national microbiology conference where we had both finished presenting papers to audiences of about a thousand. No one in their right mind would have called either of us insecure.

But on a relational and emotional level, I was immature and very insecure, and Allen was too. My whole frame of reference regarding my self-esteem was strictly based on what I could achieve academically. I truly never stopped to think about who I was, what my values were, or even what my boundaries were. It wasn't until I was in my thirties that I began to find any sort of what I call "self-wellness." And there is no way I could have a Real Love relationship with another person without even being close to having one with myself (more on this later).

LIFE USUALLY GETS WORSE BEFORE IT GETS BETTER

Anyway, there I was—twenty-three years old, single, and with a dating life that Rod Serling would have appreciated when he was stretched for ideas for new *Twilight Zone* episodes. Because of my insecurity, I was smack in the middle of having Surreal Love for the rest of my life. But as with anything that causes big changes in my love life, things had to get worse before I would wake up enough to make them better.

And get worse they did. I was about to embark on a journey that would last the rest of my life. I was about to meet my future husband. The three theories of love that I just covered definitely play an important role in explaining why I was going to fall in love with Jim, but a much more powerful theory is required to explain my decision to marry him. I needed a theory to explain why, for the first time, I had met someone that could have caused me to become emotionally devastated if he had broken up with me. When I ended things with Ken and Allen, I didn't feel too much of anything except a need to move on (to what or whom, I had no idea, but moving on sounded pretty good). I needed some explanation as to why, whenever a man I was dating would try to show Real Love for me, I would always sabotage the relationship and run like a scared rabbit.

In hindsight, I'm pretty sure this last theory is the only one powerful enough to cause me to get married out of Surreal Love. This last theory has to do with fear, baggage, social and biological clocks, and reptilian brains—romance at its finest! I call this the I.D.I.O.T. theory. It took my Surreal, Twilight Zone ability to love to new lows. But if you've ever looked at the guy you fell in love with and also mumbled, "Gee, was I an idiot," then come on board. This next theory definitely applies to you, too.

2

Any Woman Can O.D. on Surreal Love

I.D.I.O.T. WOMAN GOES TO A DOCTOR TO FIND WHOLENESS!

It seems silly now, but at the time, I had no idea why I fell totally in love with this adorable chemistry research assistant named Jim Montgomery. My feelings for Jim were more powerful and addicting than any feelings I had experienced with any other man. It wasn't until many years later that I learned the reason I fell in love with my husband. I was an I.D.I.O.T. Even though it sounds demeaning, I mean it with all my heart. Being able to identify, recognize, accept, and heal through understanding this theory is the beginning step in gaining control of your life and empowering yourself to have purposeful Real Love.

I.D.I.O.T. Theory

I = Internal cues
D = Damn cute
I = Identification with the familiar
O = Old brain
T = Timing

It took me many years, but I finally learned that the I.D.I.O.T. theory is an exquisite combination of factors that eventually put my soul through the journey of a lifetime—and believe me, this was the longest, hardest, most difficult journey of my life. Once I started on it, however, I was gifted with knowing how to live and love with Real Love by using my more evolved "new" brain to help me understand and acknowledge what my primitive, old brain was up to. Learning to help my old and new brain kiss, make up, and become friends that could work together has enabled me to build a purposeful relationship with my hubby. This knowledge has helped me keep building towards a wholeness and completeness that has given me the potential to fall head and heart in love with my man for all of the right reasons and understand the kind of "lead" I needed to develop in order to keep us committed to each other. Let me explain.

I = Internal Cues
Internal cues are powerful internal feelings aroused by fear that comes from internal and external forces—mainly societal and biological expectations. Acting or reacting in response to a

"fear-driven" instead of a "love-driven" need erodes a relationship. The cues are caused by both internal and external forces. An example of an internal force would be our "biological clocks," that very scary and extremely uncomfortable feeling— "I am running out of time to have a baby." Another example would be our "sex" hormone levels. As you will see, our biological clocks are based on old brain primal fears. Primal, reptilian brain fears are never a good reason to fall in love. As you've seen, my internal fears of not being accepted played a huge role in my falling in love for very poor reasons.

An external force causing an internal cue would be something like pressure from family, friends, and society to date and get married. Such pressure can create tremendous feelings of internal fear—fear of not "fitting in," of waiting until it's too late, of people thinking you are unwanted, strange, or whatever. The fears can go on and on. I realized that I could not live my life through fear and have any chance of being healthy and happy. There is absolutely no way that loving through fear can ever result in intimacy and Real Love. As I learned much later, the more whole I became, the less I would live and love through a fear level. Fear will always produce Surreal Love. As I learned how to reduce my fearful feelings, I slowly became able to fall in Real Love.

D = Damn Cute

Oh yeah! One of the reasons I fell in Surreal Love is that I tended to fall for men who seemed to me to be the cutest damn things I had ever seen in my entire life. And, the deeper I fell in love, the cuter he would get. Loving a man, whether you're loving him for all the wrong reasons or all the right ones, always makes him absolutely gorgeous in your eyes.

The reason I mention this to you as a part of the I.D.I.O.T. theory is it's important to keep in mind that he will look just as cute to you whether you are in Real or Surreal Love. As we continue, just realize that no matter who it is you are falling in love with, if you haven't begun working towards your own wholeness and building Real Love, you better wear your shades until you do or you could end up as blind as a bat.

As I look back at my life through the eyes of Real Love, I can see now that Ken would have absolutely no appeal to me if I were to meet him today. And my half-date who was so kind to me the evening of the Ken party is gorgeous in my memory.

Even though I have learned a lot about myself through being aware of how internal cues and "beauty in the eye of the beholder" influenced when and who I loved, it was through digging deep into the recesses of my brain and looking at the most powerful parts of the I.D.I.O.T. theory that I realized what I would have to do to have Real Love in my present relationship.

By the way, my husband has given me permission to share with you the I.D.I.O.T. stuff I had to deal with concerning him. At least I think I have his permission. In all honesty, I really still don't believe he has the emotionally evolved capacity to actually understand what he has consented to. But, as he so eloquently put it, "Yeah, yeah, sure—write what you want—just don't try to explain it all to me again" seems good enough to me. However, regarding other people who have been or are a part of my life, I want to say:

Dear family, teachers, schoolmates, friends, ex-boyfriends, etc.,

Any reference to people, places, incidents, or events portrayed herein are used to help the reader understand the importance and significance of one's past to one's present and future. All of you were and are "perfect" because you loved me the best you knew how.

Thank you.

I = Identification with the Familiar

One of the doorways to understanding why you fell in love with your guy can be opened by knowing and understanding as much as you can about your childhood and past relationships. Surreal Love can occur when you fall in love with a man who has traits inherently familiar to you. You do this because even though these traits may be pretty lousy, they are at least familiar and comfortable and a known entity. But, of course, it is these same traits that will be the ones you will find irritating and almost impossible to live with later on in your relationship.

For example, maybe your father always hid at the office or behind a newspaper or golf club. This is what's familiar to you and this increases the odds that you will be attracted to someone with similar traits. One day you will look at your beloved and wonder how you could have fallen for a guy who's such a couch potato or maybe a mouse potato or married to his work.

Or, possibly your mother was more involved with her own life or your father's or your brother's than she was with yours. This non-involvement is what you were used to. You could easily fall for a man who involved himself only in his own interests, even while he professed adoration of you. The reason is this: It is easy to love a man who has all the familiar traits of your main caregiver. Everything feels so comfortable because this is all you have ever known about love. Then one day this man announces that he loves you. You! Wow! Suddenly you are totally in love with him.

Or, a woman may fall in love with a man very much like her father. Perhaps, you grew up with a father who never gave you unconditional love. So under the "identification with the familiar" love theory, you might fall head over heels for a man who is distant, self-centered, and controlling. But since this man is quiet or sweet or says he loves you (traits you would never associate with your father), you are certain you are in love with someone who is unlike your detached dad.

This is the paradox that guarantees Surreal Love. You fall in love by recreating your childhood through identification with the familiar and then point out different character traits of your man that fill in your childhood wounds. You feel so in love. But it is Surreal Love. Why? Because you are using Surreal Love to convince yourself that by marrying this man with these familiar characteristics, you can have a happy, healing ending. You finally feel the approval you always wanted as a child. What a feeling! You feel complete, whole, safe, and in love! This Surreal Love feels so damn good you even think you've been healed of all your past childhood and relationship problems. Surreal Love keeps you from knowing you can only begin true healing by working through your own wounds.

Fortunately, identification with the familiar can also work as a positive. If your caregivers, teachers, etc. gave you a childhood of nurturing, cherishing, and unconditional love, not only have you been blessed with "off the charts" self-esteem, but you will also inherently seek these familiar traits in a mate. Being cherished is what you are used to and what you will expect from your man.

I know there are a zillion exceptions to everything I say, but that does not mean you should ignore the message. The message is this: In learning about and knowing myself, I had to look closely at all the positives and negatives that are and have been familiar to me throughout my life. In being aware of the positive traits that are familiar to me, I continually and actively seek support and nurture those same traits that are in my husband. In other words, one of the causes of Surreal Love is when "Identification with the Familiar" does a double whammy on you. When you meet a man that has traits with which you are familiar *and* traits that you are missing and need to fill in to help you be whole—BAM! Perfect Surreal Love!

By acknowledging the negatives you have become used to, you can use this new awareness to keep from being attracted to negative familiarity. Awareness is all it takes. Now you can consciously stop yourself from being unconsciously attracted to obnoxious traits in men. As you will see in this book, I learned to instantly recognize the emotional negatives of my man, get his attention concerning them, circumvent or stop the behaviors, make him feel pretty good about it, and have some fun.

O = Old Brain

Let me try to briefly (and very unscientifically) explain the concept of your "old brain." Basically, your brain has two separate parts, the old brain and the new brain. Your old brain developed millions of years ago. Think survival! The old brain oversees the basic functions of reproduction, breathing, and self-preservation through "fight or flight." It scans the environment and asks, "Am I safe?" In the old brain, instinct and powerful emotions rule. Your old brain wants you to find the mate who will ensure your survival and that of your progeny by protecting and providing. It tells you that physical appearance, prowess in either muscle or finance, and social standing are respected by your clan and tribe and provide safety by ensuring your continued belonging. Your old brain, for the sake of your survival, buried you in unconsciousness to hide the apathy, grief, fear, anger, and pain that might have, if you had expressed it, endangered your safety. Falling in love using only your old brain always results in Surreal Love.

This old brain was totally appropriate when we lived in cave condominiums and needed men to slay the wooly mammoth for a midnight snack. Today, however, our survival needs have grown beyond the physical ones of food, shelter, and clothing. Now, as we look for ways to satisfy mental, emotional, and spiritual needs and to find a partner for this endeavor, we need to employ our new brain. In other words, just because so many men act like they still live in the Stone Age doesn't mean that you have to love like Wilma Flintstone. Wake up to the modern world! The "I just want to survive" type of love should be a thing of the old brain's ancient past. We have let technology get light years ahead of our love skills. Our "lovology" has stayed in the Dark Ages because we are still loving like our ancestors did, by only loving with our old brain, getting married, and then using our new brain to finally ask, "Why am I so unhappy?" Our "new brain" is conscious, alert, logical, rational, and creative. The new brain must be engaged in order to live life from the healing level of love. To fall in Real Love we must learn not to react out of old brain responses. Here comes the take home message that my new brain is going to give you. Real Love requires recognizing old brain messages, then using your new brain to understand these messages, work through your feelings, and heal to the point where you can have Real Love for you and then develop Real Love for your partner. This is the gift this book gives you: help out of the darkness of Surreal Love into the ever-shining light of Real Love. Let's begin with recognizing old brain messages.

There's No Suitcase Big Enough to Carry Old Brain Baggage
First of all, the old brain's claim to fame is its huge overhead storage compartment. Believe me, it can hold more baggage than the Boeing Corporation ever dreamed of. Where does all this baggage come from? Baggage does not mean your pet dog or your children from a previous marriage. Baggage is the stuff from our past that we have not dealt with or worked through. Whether baggage is from childhood needs that were not met or past relationships or incidences, it always leaves an old brain fear of not feeling safe that must be worked through only by *you*. Otherwise, this baggage goes along with you on dates, down the wedding aisle, on your honeymoon—you name it, that baggage will be there, keeping you in Surreal Love.

For example, hopefully when you were about a year and a half old, your core needs for beginning autonomy and independence were met. When you climbed off your loving, caring parent's lap to explore for the first time in the next room, you were hugged and told to have fun and that Mommy or Daddy would be right there if you needed something. This parent let you know that independence was acceptable, but provided a safety net just in case you needed to be reassured.

But if you had an insecure, overprotective parent, he or she may have denied your autonomy and independence by telling you in so many words to be careful, watch out, or you might get hurt. This parent gave you a clear message that you could not handle going in the other room by yourself without them being there to watch you. From this experience you would pick up some baggage of dependence and fear to carry with you into every future relationship. You may recognize this kind of baggage if you have a fear of being engulfed whenever anyone tries to get too close to you. Your fear of not being allowed to be independent overrides your need for emotional closeness. You may unconsciously push the person away even though you really love him.

Or the opposite could have occurred. Your parent may have been distant and self-centered. You would have sat in this parent's lap but been told to stop clinging, to go away, and to quit being a pest. You would have gone exploring to fill the empty place inside you. The baggage you pick up from this experience will probably manifest as an insatiable need for closeness and feelings of abandonment and rejection. You want you and your partner to do everything together, and even if your partner is just a few minutes late, you feel abandoned. Inside this baggage is still the little girl who needed more time on Mommy's or Daddy's lap.

You picked up more baggage at school, at church or synagogue, and in your social group. To be safe, to be accepted, and to be loved you had to lose or repress parts of yourself. You learned to not express your anger, to deny your sensuality, to submit rather than assert, to deny your needs in favor of the needs of others, and so on. You survived, fragmented but alive. As you grew up and created relationships outside your family, you carried these unmet fears and needs and sought out people who you believed could meet them (and of course, they sought you out for the same reason!).

Two Halves Do Not Make a Whole!

Just like your man has no notion of time beyond Monday Night Football, your old brain has no sense of linear time. Today, tomorrow, and yesterday do not exist in your old brain. Everything that was still is, just as it was when it happened—that same sense of fear, abandonment, and rejection. Sometimes you have feelings within your relationship that are alarmingly out of proportion to the events that triggered them. For example, you might be reading a good book, thinking warm, loving thoughts about your partner. You decide to call him on the phone at work. He does not answer. Your rational mind can list ten reasons why he does not pick up the phone, but your old brain feels abandoned. You are an educated, sophisticated woman feeling as vulnerable as when your mother left you with an unfamiliar baby-sitter.

You were born whole, with both old and new brain intact. Even though the new one was not fully developed, they worked in harmony to make sure that you felt safe and protected physically (old brain) and spiritually and emotionally (new brain). Your old brain insures your physical safety, even at the cost of splitting off from your new brain. Your new brain embraces risks, limitless possibility, creative exploration, enthusiasm, and wholeness. Your brain never forgets the perfection of your "Original Wholeness"—that total communion with the universe you experienced at birth. In those first moments of life, your soul felt a sense of oneness, wholeness, a primitive spiritually, a feeling so beautiful and blissful that you strive to regain it throughout life. To be able to have Real Love, *you* have to do the work necessary to heal your woundedness and get the educational, business, financial, etc. acumen to make your primitive, survival instinct brain feel safe. Only then will it send an "all clear" message to your new brain and give you the gift of seeing a potential partner logically and rationally. In other words, you can fall in love with the Real attributes of your loved one. If you don't do this yourself, you are doomed to Surreal Love. Your old brain will be determined to restore your wholeness by finding the "right partner" to complete you and make you feel safe and whole.

How does this information add up to our understanding of romantic attraction? In concise terms, childhood baggage is a biggie! Unless you have dealt with it and figured out all those old brain reactions that you experience daily in your life, you will fall in love using only your old brain, and this, as I said before, is the main reason so many marriages fail.

Most of us enter relationships with the expectation that our partners will magically restore this feeling of "Original Wholeness." But your partner cannot meet this need. Failure to understand this truth leads inevitably to unhappiness with your relationship. I'll say it again and again: Only *you* can provide your wholeness. Only *you* can use your "new brain" to sort through your baggage of fractured wholeness and begin the healing process of developing and finding the lost parts of who you really are. Only *you* can provide the safety and security that your old brain wants.

Use your new brain to recognize when your old brain is sending you a message, what the message is, why it is there, and what you can do about it. By the time you finish the book, you will be able to feel these old brain messages of fear, sex, anxiety, Surreal Love, etc., understand them, and heal them. Otherwise, your old brain will be on a continuous "search and find" mission to try to restore "original wholeness" through a man. And if he offers familiarity from your childhood and has the missing pieces that you don't have, your old brain screams that you are "in love." Your old brain, through this other person, recreates your childhood environment and fills in the open wounds. Feeling whole makes you feel love like you have never felt before. But remember, your partner is only giving you an illusory sense of wholeness. Relationships fail when you're "in love" but not whole. The only true way to recapture wholeness is to develop the missing traits yourself. Search within yourself for the strengths and abilities and love you are lacking. Real Love requires being strong enough to always work towards wholeness.

T = *Timing*

Timing is an often-overlooked factor in falling in love. It is beautifully described by Dr. Judith Sills in her book *A Fine Romance*. Even though "timing" is stimulated by external forces, it is an internal process acting as a psychological catalyst for commitment. You may have had many relationships, but suddenly it is time. You are ready (or think you are) for a lifetime commitment. When the time is right, no matter who the particular partner is, you tend to fall in love. The problem is that "timing" is usually inspired by the head, not the heart. External forces such as finishing college, one of you moving to another state, or finally becoming financially secure, can make "timing" an artificial reason to seek a serious relationship. As you may suspect, falling in love only because it is time to do so is likely to result in an unhappy, unfulfilled relationship.

GIRL FINDS SURREAL LOVE AT ITS FINEST!

Okay, it's time to take another look back to my dating life, in particular, to the part about how I went from dating Jim to actually marrying him.

Jim and I dated steadily for over five years. Our dating life was about as Surreal as dating could possibly be. During the first couple of years, we were both at the same university. He was trying to get into medical school and I was pursuing a master's degree in microbiology. We continued to date for three more years while Jim was in medical school in Memphis and I was working on a doctorate in Knoxville, five hundred miles away.

There is no question that I fell in love with Jim under the I.D.I.O.T. theory, although the other theories certainly played a role. He definitely was a combination of "Me Tarzan" and "Larry King Live." He was a brilliant premed student who was going to be a doctor with plenty of social prestige and lots of money. My status and self-esteem were definitely elevated by this. But to fall in love enough to marry him, now we're talking powerful Surreal Love completely based in the I.D.I.O.T. theory. In order to tell the story right, I've got to give you the I.D.I.O.T. letters out of order, but this is how they happened.

Jim is damn cute. He was, is, and always will be the best-looking man I have ever seen. The minute he walked into my German class, I remember asking myself, "Why can't I get somebody like him?" He looked perfect. I loved the way he carried himself in his long, lean blue jeans, cowboy boots, and white T-shirt with five holes in it. As I stared at him, I was sitting at my desk, wearing blue polyester pants and a fresh white blouse. My old brain was already yelling at me—"Here's a missing piece that Cheryl needs to be whole. This man isn't afraid to be different. This man likes to be noticed. This man doesn't care if his clothes aren't what everybody likes. He has self-expression, Cheryl. You've always been afraid to have it and you need it to be whole. So let's take the quickest, easiest, surreal path and fill in your fractures with this man!"

My fear of self-expression was always an old brain reaction. Because of past experiences, I was fearful of being criticized, laughed at, or not accepted. Of course, I didn't know any of this back then, so this part of my wholeness was fractured and unhealed. My new brain didn't stand a chance. My old brain was in total control of my love life.

You can bet that all internal cues were firmly in place by the time I was twenty-five. I can remember actually standing in my apartment and saying to myself, "Okay, Cheryl. You will have your doctorate in three months. Now, what relationship status are you most comfortable with for the rest of your life:

> Dr. Cheryl McClary—never married
>
> Dr. Cheryl McClary—married
>
> Dr. Cheryl McClary—divorced

Then I made a concrete decision that it was too socially fearful for me to take a chance that I might never get married if I didn't marry Jim on March 19th as expected. I could not bear the thought of going through life as a "spinster," "single woman," or an "old maid." The fear of never getting married was one I couldn't handle. Whereas the thought of getting married and then, if it didn't work, getting a divorce sounded like a piece of cake. My internal cue to be married or divorced, but not "never been married," was one my old brain could not or would not resist. Jim was my answer.

How I wish I had known then what you will learn from the next two chapters: how to look to yourself, and only yourself, to answer and confront internal cues produced by society. Biologically, I wasn't too fearful. Having children wasn't one of my priorities when I was in my twenties. But, socially, it never occurred to me that my fear of being "never married" was one that I needed to resolve by using my new brain, not by getting married.

Through Jim, I totally identified with three dominant familiar traits that were common to people who were important to me throughout different times of my childhood, adolescence, and dating years. He was extremely intelligent, self-centered, and distant. But, just as my new brain was trying to be rational and cause me to begin to feel a little uncertain about the distance in our relationship, he writes "I Love You" on a paper towel and gives it to me as we're leaving a movie theater. I was brimming with Surreal Love! Here was a man who had the traits I was most familiar and most comfortable with, yet he could write that he loved me. What a gap this filled in! I felt so fulfilled and complete through Jim.

Distance and love, distance and love, distance and love. I was thrilled that a way had been found for someone else to try to heal the distance I had experienced in past relationships, yet stay distant enough not to scare me off! I didn't know then that only I could heal the space in my heart created by distant people. I didn't know that "distance and love" would be what would make us, break us, and then help me eventually find us. The authors Firestone and Catlett, in their book *Fear of Intimacy*, call this self-protective distancing "inwardness" and show how it severely restricts emotional interaction between partners.

As you'll see in your own journey, healing this distance we create within ourselves is the first step to finding closeness between women and men. But for the time being, my old brain was still in control. It was happy that we had found such an easy way out to feel wholeness. This was Surreal Love at its finest.

Surreal Love is so deceiving. It feels so powerful and strong that I just didn't pay attention to anything else, like friends, family, roommates, myself, or any and all warning signs from my new brain. I only cared about making my entire life fit around his. Among many frogs in my singles dating pond, there were actually a couple of real princes. There were guys I would date for a while who tried hard to really get to know me as a person.

These guys didn't hesitate to tell me and show me how much they cared about me. This felt so unfamiliar and uncomfortable that each time this happened I would feel distressed, apprehensive, and scared. After all, I hadn't recognized, dealt with, or tried to heal any of my baggage. My self-esteem was fractured and wounded. My love for Jim was perfect for my low level of self-confidence. The fact that Jim was emotionally distant made me love him even more for all the wrong reasons. I felt safe and secure because I knew he could always be distant enough to never really know the real me, and if he never really knew me, he would love me forever. Yes, it was a fake, Surreal Love, but it was love nonetheless and it felt so real. After all, I remember clearly thinking, How could anyone who really got to know the true me still love me?

I wish I could have used my new brain to recognize the fear-based messages of my old brain so I could have worked through them, healed enough to find Real Love for myself, and then only been attracted to men who cherished me with the Real Love I deserved and could give in return. But, alas, at that time in my life, it just wasn't meant to be. As soon as I got those feelings, I would sabotage the developing closeness by making it very clear that I never wanted to get married or have children. This worked like a charm to push away any man who had the possibility of developing a relationship of Real Love. When Jim would mention marriage or kids (just twice in five years), I reminded him I didn't want either one. He said that was fine, but he could still see us being together in the future with two Ferraris parked in the garage. Now, this was my kind of love!

Our Surreal Love relationship came into full bloom once Jim started medical school. I came fully into my own as a fake person. If Jim did something to make me angry, I didn't show it. If he did something to hurt my feelings, I kept it to myself. I was so unreal! One time I rode a Greyhound bus five hundred miles just to see him. Picture me sitting for ten hours next to a cigar-smoker who mumbled to himself every time he took a drink from his flask. As I was beginning to turn green with nausea and dizziness, I leaned my head against the window, hitting a window bar and cutting my forehead. Needless to say, this was fast becoming one of the worst trips of my life. But thankfully, I arrived at the bus terminal right on time. I could barely contain my excitement at being able to see and be with Jim as I staggered off the bus. I looked everywhere, but he wasn't there. I waited over an hour in a smoke-filled, grimy bus station. He finally showed, saying he was playing pinball and just lost track of time. I should be furious, right? But that would make him feel bad and would be uncomfortable. I'm Surreal, remember? I can't make a scene. I just tell him that's okay, not to worry. I knew medical school was hard and he needed a break, etc., etc. What a bunch of crap! But that was me at that time—a total fraud to myself, Jim, and our relationship. Remember, I was familiar with being second or third. I was comfortable being treated like this. I was an I.D.I.O.T. and I had no one to blame but myself.

Oh boy, was our surreal dating relationship dishonest. I could never tell Jim the truth about me because I didn't know my truths. I couldn't be honest with him about my feelings because I wasn't honest with myself. I didn't even know I was supposed to think about these kinds of things. A woman thinking about herself and who she is? It was unheard of. That would be downright conceited, self-serving, and even unladylike. Plus, if I learned my truths and then Jim learned about who I was—well, he might not love me anymore. That might mean I was unlovable. My worst old brain fear would be true. I didn't love myself enough to even think of dealing with this.

How inane it all seems now as I look back. But while I was dating, it was my entire life! Jim's Surreal Love for me was the only relational validation I could understand. So I concentrated on trying to make Jim's life easier since medical school was so difficult and stressful. I was oblivious to the fact that I was knocking myself out for my own doctoral degree. Jim's needs were top priority! For me to act any other way might mean Jim wouldn't love me anymore, definitely a warning sign of fully blossoming Surreal Love. Once again, this was all my own doing. When he wrote that "I love you" message on the paper towel in the movie theater, I was ready to bolt. I had become very comfortable with having the Surreal image of not needing anyone, not loving anyone, and not having anyone interfere with my career plans—ever. Jim was truly amazing about the whole thing. He would get me to write only one letter a day until I could actually write "I love you" in eight days. After about another week, I was actually able to say it and decided this meant I ought to stick around.

Problem was, I wouldn't know until years of marriage and two children later that Real Love means being able to write and say "I love you" even after you know the truths of your own and each other's hearts. Jim and I could talk about anything and everything as long as we didn't have to reveal very much about our own selves. We were a perfect Surreal match. Everything looked great on the outside, but neither one of us wanted or knew how to discover what was real on the inside.

GET ME TO THE CHURCH ON TIME

The timing was perfect. We were both ready. But I didn't know then that the only timing that is important is finding your wholeness first, then your Real Love. It was the spring break of his last semester of medical school and of my last semester of my PhD. Our Surreal Love was kickin' in full steam. My old brain was sending me a neon, brightly lit, fear-based message: "You better marry him now before he becomes a rich doctor and finds someone else!" and I played into his old brain fears by making him aware of all the positions I had applied for all over the country, which caused his old brain to send him a message: "You better marry her now or she'll move to another city and fall for some other man!"

Our fear-based love was so strong that nothing could stop us from getting married. Jim's marriage proposal was so romantic. We were riding in his "souped-up" dark green Nova listening to Aretha Franklin belt out "Chain of Fools." On our way to some fine dining at Ralph's Ranch House, we had to stop for gas at the Diamond 66 station. After Jim stuck the gas nozzle in the tank, he poked his head in the window and said, "This kind of

stuff is real hard for me, so, um, so—do ya wanna get married?"
My answer was an old-brainer—"Okay." Five months later, we
had a party at my parents' house and got married at the university chapel.

Woman Uses "Man Putty" to Feel and Look Like She Has it Together!

As my old brain continued to out-feel my new brain, I was falling
more and more in love. I know my dating life sounds weird and
my marriage was even weirder. But let's face it. Nearly all of us
were "out of it" in our own surreal worlds in one way or another.
None of us really knows what we were doing when we "fell in
love." Like everyone else, I had loads of hormones and tons of
fractures. It was so much easier to let Jim fill them in than for me
to heal them myself (plus, it never occurred to me that I could).
For example, each time Jim was assertive, spoke his mind, put his
needs first, became impatient, or stood up for himself, my surreal, old brain love would grow even deeper. These were all pieces
of me that had gotten misplaced somewhere. Pieces that only I
could find. But temporarily I was plugging up empty spaces with
man putty (appropriately named by the toy industry as "Silly
Putty"). It looked good, felt good, and worked well. Now I was a
patched-up I.D.I.O.T. who was in total Surreal Love and married
for old-brain reasons. How long would the putty hold up? What
would happen when it started to dry up, crack, and fall off?

As you will see, the putty really started crumbling after several
years of marriage. As long as I kept maintaining the relationship
status quo by blindly slapping on a fresh layer of putty, my man

was happy and our marriage "worked." It "worked" because as long as I loved like an I.D.I.O.T., ignored the wise, rational messages of my new brain, and used man putty to fill in my wounds, the relationship looked pretty good from all outward appearances. We were smiling and happy to the outside world. But this kind of marriage is false and surreal. I was living an emotionally fragile existence as I kept trying to hold myself together. This is no way to live. It is only existence.

3

Regaining Consciousness

IT'S MY MARRIAGE, I CAN CRY IF I WANT TO!

I was going through the daily motions of womanhood—working, being married, and having children. Everything seemed so perfect but, for some reason, I sometimes found myself crying silently in the shower. More and more often I felt inexplicably sad. I became so insecure in my relationship with my husband that one evening I sat on the edge of our bed and begged my husband to tell me if the reason we were drifting apart was because of the scruffy blue bathrobe I loved to wear around the house.

That's when it happened! I began regaining consciousness! My soul began having flashbacks to a time before I became fractured. For the first time, I saw myself, and I was shocked. I actually believed that my blue robe was the reason I thought Jim did not love me as much as he once did and this was why I was unhappy. I ignored the fact that we had recently moved five hundred miles away from family and friends to a new city, changed jobs, and had a baby, among hundreds of other related changes. None of these explanations occurred to me. Instead, being the "Miss Everything Must Be My Fault" woman that I was, I interpreted any unhappiness on anyone's part as somehow being a result of something I did. I believed my relationship with my husband was deteriorating because I wore a beat-up blue bathrobe and my love of this robe was responsible for my success or failure as a wife. I sat frozen to the bed and looked, without blinking, at myself and my ludicrous reasoning. A meteor of understanding exploded within me. This was not about my relationship with *him*, it was about my relationship with *me*.

SHOW ME THE WAY TO GO HOME

At that moment I chose to start the long trip home to myself. I chose me. I didn't want to be distant from myself anymore. I chose empowerment. And even better, I realized that by even just deciding to choose empowerment, I was already there.

Is the rest just detail? Yes, the "detail" is lots and lots of hard work. But anyone can do it. Keep this in mind:

- Understand your old brain messages
- Work through the emotions these old brain feelings invoke

- Discover and develop Real Love for yourself
- Heal to the level of actually having Real Love for yourself
- Heal enough to develop Real Love for him

By choosing to love and honor myself, I was choosing life and the journey to Real Love. There was no turning back. It was time to regain consciousness by resuscitating my heart with self-administered Real Love CPR. I was gaining "the lead" now. It was liberating and so clear to me. I could not change my man, but I could create change. I could change me. I could cause a behavior change in him, and I could change the dynamics of our relationship. The key word here was *me*. I was the one who wanted positive changes in our relationship. I had to focus on me first and him second so that I could get what I wanted and I was ready to take him on!

The day of my "blue bathrobe enlightenment," I got up from the bed and headed straight for a hot bath. I needed to think (for some reason, I do all my serious thinking in or around water—the tub, shower, the ocean, a pool, rain). I began looking at the patterns of my childhood and young adulthood that I had brought into my relationship. I saw how over and over I allowed the people in my life that I cared about to get their way, no matter how deeply I disagreed with them. I realized how many pieces of myself I had lost throughout the years because I wanted to be a "good little girl." I had lost the ability to stand up for what I believed. I had lost the ability to get angry and show it, to get really mad, to yell, be silly, to say what I wanted, to even know what I wanted. Even though I have now spent years finding and reclaiming these parts of me, that bathtub revelation made me feel like a new person.

I am amazed at how many years I operated through fear. I was afraid to make anyone mad, afraid of my hidden anger, afraid to speak my mind, afraid of never having another relationship, afraid of a loss of income, afraid of not being Mrs. Somebody, afraid of divorce. I had to learn that to stay committed to Jim, I must never, ever be afraid of being uncomfortable, embarrassed, hurt, or even laughed at by my husband or anyone else, or afraid of the need to be committed.

The "blue robe incident" woke me up. To what? I wasn't sure. For what? I was sure. It was with complete clarity that I knew I had to figure out what Real Love was all about! This was totally up to me to do.

I had to take control of the situation. I was the one who was unhappy. I was the one who wanted a better relationship. I was the one who was maintaining the "status-quo dead zone" of marital Surreal Love. I was sick of it! And if I didn't do something, I was going to get even sicker from soul suffocation.

IS HE AN ARMADILLO OR A KNIGHT?

The first thing I had to do was assess the "situation." I had one young son and another on the way. I wanted to stay committed, to stay married to the same man who was their father. I wanted to have Real Love with *him*. This led me to the first question I had to answer. Who was he? What was it about my husband that was so irritating and totally "out of it" when it came to having "relationship moments"? I sat down and made a list of the traits he had that made me crazy at times. The list was as follows:

- He is in touch with his feelings only when he gets a headache.
- He believes his "feminine side" refers to his maternal relatives.
- He thinks *The Celestine Prophecy* is a topless dancer on Bourbon Street.
- He assumes *The Road Less Traveled* is the interstate under construction.
- He thinks a "soul mate" is a Motown hit from the sixties.
- He has developed self-centeredness into a fine art.
- He thinks "childhood baggage" is what kids take to slumber parties and summer camp.
- He thinks he is "emotionally available" if he has a cellular phone.
- He thinks "inner guidance" is what steers a cruise missile.
- He refuses to read *Men Are from Mars, Women Are from Venus* because he has no time for science fiction.
- He experiences enlightenment only when the lights flicker after a power outage.
- He thinks "over accommodation" means the hotel is overbooked.
- He escapes into couch or mouse potato mode and channel surfs away to TV or computer land just when you need him most.

In summary, maybe your man is from Mars, but mine is definitely from Pluto. It wouldn't surprise me at all to learn that there is armadillo life on Pluto. I was in love with a guy who was a master at keeping enough distance between us to keep us from having Real Love. And I was the one who was continually allowing it to happen. Even when he wasn't keeping his distance by hiding behind the remote or the computer, I believed he had "distance devices" on him at almost all times.

I realized that Jim wore an invisible shield of armor, allowing him to believe if he hid his fears and failures, he was invulnerable to hurt, abandonment, and rejection. He really believes that if he lets his shield down and shows his feelings, he will be judged "unmanly." I believe that most men make sure you see their protective shield: a business suit, a white coat, a police uniform. They may even wear or carry "weapons" to defend themselves from emotional feelings—helmets, badges, stethoscopes, power drills, chain saws—all signs of their struggle to maintain distance and stay in control. I knew that this shield my husband wore was one of the ways of keeping me from living and loving honestly. How in the world was I going to have Real Love and break through all this "man stuff"? Hmm—man stuff—that's it! I had to figure out what I expected from my man and quit being disappointed that he wasn't living up to some unrealistic standard.

He's just a man for chrissakes! Society has done a real number on me and on him. As I said earlier, politically correct wisdom led me to believe I couldn't be happy with a man unless he had a good job, was adorable, funny, witty, a great conversationalist, terrific father material, my most perfect friend, great in bed, and—most important of all—my soul mate.

Dream on! There's no way anyone can be all of these things. But the reality of the situation is this: I love having him in my life. I love the fact that we have children, and I hope we'll have grandchildren together.

He's just a man. And he doesn't cotton to change. Only I could make him and the relationship come alive. He can fix cars, sinks, lawnmowers, CD players, and commodes, but he cannot fix himself or our relationship. He is completely clueless. If he can't touch, smell, taste, hear, or see something, then it doesn't exist. Feelings? Emotional availability? Relationships? These things don't relate at all to the five senses. So he has no idea what I'm talking about, much less how to fix them.

It was going to be up to me to find the emotional, romantic life and pulse of our marriage. I had the "knowing" it would take to find Real Love. So how was I going to do it? I was going to take control.

It was time for me to get my act together and take control of myself and my relationship. Through all my experience as a single woman, professor, attorney, and wife, I have learned that I can change and control only one thing—*me*. But I also know that by changing and controlling me, I can change and control my relationship. I had the power to develop and nurture his human qualities of kindness, goodness, decency, and loving me for who I am. This ability is a beautiful gift that has been given to women. And, while you are implementing this book, if your partner remains "teachable enough" to learn to eventually cherish you and your gift to the relationship, then you will be alive as you never have been before. You will love how great it feels!

WHO NEEDS A RELATIONSHIP ANYWAY?

After making my list of Jim's problem traits, I thought about why I really want a relationship. Life is a gift from a power much greater than us. This same higher power has chosen to put woman and man *together* on the *same* planet. Why? Because when a woman and a man truly create Real Love with and between each other, it provides an unprecedented, unparalleled, unequalled, glorious opportunity for mutual growth, fulfillment, self-expression, and enthusiasm for life!

It is through your relationships that your life gives your soul the only opportunity to experience your highest version of your *self*. Don't waste this gift of life by just settling for existence. Living your life with enthusiasm is the key to finding and living through your soul. Wake up and enthusiastically live as many minutes of your life as you can. There ain't nothing that can wake up your soul more profoundly than a Real relationship with a man!

TAKE A POWER WALK

I had to actually talk out loud to myself and tell myself what to do. I told my husband and kids that I was going for a long walk and I didn't know how long it would take. I needed to be alone. The last words I heard from them as I walked out the door were "But what are we going to eat for dinner?" For the first time in their lives and mine, I did not know or care. Change was in the air!

As I walked and walked, I told myself, Cheryl, you are the unhappy one. Jim is completely happy. He just wants everything to stay the same, which means I keep doing all I can to please him and make his happiness my main goal in life. No wonder he's so damn content! I would be, too. I am going to have to be the change agent. I have to figure out a way to show him how to enjoy intimacy without feeling threatened and controlled. I must help him be a compassionate human being. My soul had finally gotten my attention enough to help me see that I needed to make the choices to begin true emotional healing.

As I continued walking and talking to myself, I realized that if I changed, the dynamics of my relationship would have to change, and this would definitely produce a change in his behavior. My ability to change is the greatest power in my relationship. I just didn't know it until then. It was such a great feeling knowing that having Real Love with Jim was up to me. This was doable. I had no intention of letting myself down.

Step 1. The first step towards Real Love was understanding how and why Surreal Love played such a large role in our falling in love. This was the beginning of me trying to understand who I was and what I needed to learn in order to find Real Love and wholeness.

Step 2. The second step was for me to become strong and whole enough to do what needed to be done to "take the lead" in our relationship in order to progress to my goals of happiness, wholeness, commitment, and Real Love.

Step 3. The third step was that once I was empowered enough to take on anything, especially Real Love for myself, I knew I was ready to make a relationship that was worth being committed to. I was primed and ready. It was time to learn how to quit loving in I.D.I.O.T. mode and learn to re-fall in love with Jim for all the new brain, right, logical reasons, especially the return of joy and enthusiasm to our marriage. As I walked back up my driveway, I formulated my action plan. I knew what I had to do and I didn't care if it took days or years. I just knew I had to do it and there was no turning back. This felt too right and too good. A woman must *always* trust this feeling.

Step-by-Step

If I had to summarize what I learned at that point in my life, this is what I would say:

- I learned to take the lead.
- I learned to follow my innate desire to regain wholeness by listening to my heart, not my head.
- I kept reminding myself that I was whole at birth and had the power to reclaim my wholeness. Then I trusted myself. The big picture was scary, but I only had to take one step at a time.
- I became aware of my tendencies to give my power and self-determination to others, particularly to men. This awareness jump-started the journey to wholeness.

- I called up all the strength and courage I could muster and ventured into the exploration of my childhood patterns and relationships. Before I could leave them behind, I had to recognize them.
- I understood that as I searched for the True Me, I did not need to make any conscious changes in my relationship. As I changed, the relationship changed on its own accord. I learned how to fall in love again with the same person in a new and healthy way.
- I was not afraid to ask for help and support from friends, mentors, counselors, and therapists.

Falling in love using your new brain will help you love yourself and live in Real Love for the right reasons. Engaging your new brain will empower you with the inner resources to face your partner. You can become the catalyst to help him become human by taking care of yourself first. To learn to be truly human, a man must bond with a woman (you). To begin this bonding process, he must let down his invisible shield, but he will probably never remove the shield on his own. He is clueless and happy being clueless. You are the one who wants the relationship to be better. Therefore, you are the one who is going to have to do it. By becoming whole yourself, his shield will begin to disintegrate. He needs you to model what a whole and complete person is. Then, through your love for him, you can teach him that a *real* man is a hu*man*.

MEN DON'T COTTON TO CHANGE, BUT WOMEN DO

This book will not change your mate, but it will help you teach him to realize that he can choose to be more of a human being. You can help him relearn what came naturally to him as a small boy—how to emotionally connect with those he loves. And, in your teaching, you will be affirming who you are, what you stand for, and what you deserve. For you to be effective, you must believe to the core of your being that you deserve to be loved and to be happy in your relationship with yourself as well as with him.

The road to wholeness is not an easy road, but if you travel with your sense of humor it need not be a terrifying one. One of the hardest steps in developing your wholeness, and therefore your self-respect, is the difficult discovery that you have responsibilities in this relationship. Your key responsibility is to develop, first and foremost, a loving relationship with yourself. This book is devoted to helping you understand and care for yourself so that you will be healthy in *all* your relationships for the rest of your life. You can't just choose to leave your relationship. Unless you choose to heal and become whole, you will simply bring the same issues into the next relationship. As you've learned, unless you choose wholeness first, you will fall "in love with" the same type of guy again and again—different man, same issues. Also, you can't simply recognize that your partner is clueless and blame him for letting you down and making you unhappy. You may be sad or unhappy, but *your* life is what *you* make it, not what he makes it.

Wife Must Assume Responsibility for Her Sanity

Assuming responsibility means the difficult task of facing your own fears, overcoming them, and learning to live your life through the emotion of love. You may be afraid of asking him certain questions, of being yourself around him, of losing an identity deeply associated with him (the doctor's wife, the plumber's helper, the jock's cheerleader). You may need to start small and take baby steps toward healing emotionally. Don't give up! You owe yourself this gift of living authentically. Any moment of your life that you touch with love begins a healing process.

You have the courage to acknowledge, face, and overcome your fears with wisdom and respect for who you are. Always pay attention to your feelings so you can make better choices. Only then can you hope to stay whole while in a relationship. Your man can learn to relate in a manner that makes you feel great about yourself when you are with him *and* when you are not. Your relationship with yourself matters more than your relationship with him or anyone else. This gives you the power to love yourself, which, in turn, may empower you to accept and continue to love your man. Implementing what you learn from this book may not save your marriage or suddenly produce a warm, loving, beautiful relationship. But, for the first time in your history together, you may be able to open up the following possibilities:

- You will stop allowing him to have so much power over how you feel about yourself.

- The self-confidence and strength you exhibit may produce positive behavior changes in your partner which, in turn, may enable him to bond with you instead of only with himself.
- As you make relationship decisions with the awareness of what is best for you, you may see his true colors for the first time. You may slowly but surely come to the realization that it is your soul's desire to have a relationship that is real and human. How you respond to this may be "life-giving" for you.
- Your man may actually start to let down his invisible shield and begin to "feel." This can open up a world of opportunities for the two of you, from getting to know each other for the first time to getting professional relationship healing, in the form of counseling, therapy, or relationship seminars (i.e., from folks who actually know what they're doing).
- You may enable him to make the choices necessary to be more present and loving in his relationship with you.

Getting There Is Half the Fun

Try not to focus on results or outcomes. Concentrate on the process. Enjoy each little moment of growth, strength, and change—of finding you and each other. Always remember that like most men, yours is probably not beyond help. He simply is a man.

Recognize that at some deep level he sees himself through your eyes. Like you, he honestly needs to feel that he is loved and cherished as a person, not just as a paycheck, a protector, a position in society, and so on. Look for the potential "humanness" hidden inside him. As you become whole you can make him feel loved, manly, and appreciated when he feels unsure, depressed, silly, or tearful. When he argues, pouts, or resorts to the silent treatment or other acting out behaviors, recognize that he is filled with an inner conflict he does not understand. He is struggling to connect with those he loves and with the parts of himself he lost on the way to manhood—tenderness, vulnerability, neediness. His repeated attempts to disconnect are bumbling efforts to regain the connection to humanness he lost a long time ago. In other words, while you are journeying toward Real Love, try to remember that a little compassion goes a long way in nurturing commitment. (Time to take a five-second entrance exam to be sure you are ready for the next section. Just circle the correct answer in the right-hand column.)

Entrance Exam for Real Love (I)

Surreal Love Is:	Example
Deceiving	Ken
	Me
Dangerous	Ken
	Me

Dishonest	Allen
	Me
Fear-Based	Jim
	Me
Using Your Old Brain	Jim
	Me
Doomed Relationship	Ken, Allen, Jim
	Me

Please read this and write the correct answer in the space below: Question I–Can you identify the common denominator in each of the examples of Surreal Love?

Answer: _____

If you answered "Me," you passed the first half of your Entrance Exam. As you can see, my dating fiascos and the troubled parts of my marriage had nothing to do with men, and everything to do with me and my lack of self-wellness.

Entrance Exam for Real Love (II)

Real Love Is:	Example
Honest	Jim
	Me

Safe	Jim
	Me
Using Your New Brain	Jim
	Me
Purposeful	Jim
	Me
Self-Wellness Based	Me
	Me
Wholeness	Me
	Me

Please read this and write the correct answer in the space below: Question II–Can you identify the common denominator in each of the examples of Real Love?

Answer: _____

If you answered "Me," you have now passed the entire Entrance Exam for Real Love. Once again, it was entirely up to *me* to have Real Love through self-wellness. Knowing this is the way to keep love and men in the proper perspective and priority. The perspective is that they are just men and they can be absolutely wonderful, but they cannot complete you or make you whole. They will not find Real Love and bring it to you on their own. They cannot fill in your missing pieces. You must make yourself the Top Priority. Finding Real Love through following the path to self-wellness is the top priority. Raising yourself to this level will move the entire relationship closer to finding Real Love.

Now that you understand what Real Love is all about, you have taken a huge step towards self-wellness. Keep going for it! Whether single, married, divorced, or widowed, it is always miraculous when a woman regains her enthusiasm for living and loving as she embraces her gift of self-discovery. I want this book to give you the knowledge necessary to develop, define, and refine your strong sense of self. With this knowledge you can spend the rest of your life secure in who you are, and fall or stay in Real Love with your man for the right reasons.

In the next section you will see my strategy for becoming emotionally "self-well." It was hard work, but, quite frankly, I love the gift I was giving myself. With a little creativity, I was able to come up with ways to start becoming whole no matter how busy my schedule was. Self-wellness is definitely the "gift that keeps on giving."

{SECTION II}

Take Charge to Love, Honor, and Cherish Thyself

4

The Price You Pay for Finding You Is—Love

NO MAN CAN MAKE A WOMAN FEEL INFERIOR WITHOUT HER PERMISSION

I was getting closer to understanding why my relationship was based on and actively existing in Surreal Love. The "blue robe" incident had brought me out of marriage unconsciousness. My long walk had empowered me to see the reality of my marriage. Part of this reality was that I had implicitly given my husband permission to make me feel inferior in our marriage. I never complained about it; I just felt it every time I couldn't live up to his expectation of who or what I was supposed to be and when I was supposed to be it. In other words, I would begin to doubt myself, and self-doubt will prevent self-wellness every time.

Houston, We Have a Problem

To begin working through my stuff, I had to look at my relationship in a whole new way. In other words, I needed to identify what my expectations were for us. I had to acknowledge what it was I needed from our marriage and to lay out what I thought were the problems we were having. So I did just that and wrote it in a letter to Jim. I gave it to him on Friday night after dinner and it felt great. Jim calls it my "Houston, we have a problem" letter. He takes me so seriously—yeah, right. Anyway, I was inspired by a letter published by a reader in Dr. Christiane Northrup's *Women's Bodies, Women's Wisdom*, so I revised it to be my own heartfelt message. The first step of working through my stuff and taking the lead with Jim began like this:

Dear Handsome Husband,

I am not happy. My heart yearns for connection. My greatest grief is when my loss of emotional connection with you seems to come at the cost of connection to myself. I become dead inside when I try to conform to the person you would rather me be again. I cannot be the "walled-off," closed up, agreeable woman I used to be. When the natural compassion, openness, caring of my heart becomes distorted and usurped, I lose my sense of aliveness and enthusiasm. I am left feeling empty and drained. It takes an incredible amount of energy to shape one's self to fit someone else's need for distance and non-vulnerability. But no matter how tempting it is for me to conform in the hope of gaining your love, or of feeling safe, it costs me too much to be in a hierarchy when my heart is begging for partnership, connection, and intimacy. I see this cost in the faces of too many couples—the suppressed anger or the deadness that resides there. That can't be the way marriage is supposed to be. I won't let it.

Love,
Cheryl

Jim read the letter, looked up, and in all seriousness said, "Cheryl, I am very impressed. Your handwriting has really improved."

Hello—anybody home? I couldn't believe he said that—even worse, he was proud of himself for the remark! As I stared at him, I tried to look back at my relationship and figure out what in the world I had been doing over the last ten years. Without even taking time to blink, I saw all the signs that I had been living a partnership of Surreal Love. The following list flashed in front of me like a Las Vegas billboard:

- I was over-accommodating to everyone I cared about.
- I had difficulty setting limits regarding my time, energy, health, and love.
- I was usually passive and uncomplaining.
- I was the peacemaker and harmonizer in my relationship.
- I put the needs of everyone I cared about before my own.
- I had a low opinion of myself, which was hidden from everyone, including myself.
- I thought I did not have the right to be angry.
- I was a reflection of the man with whom I was in a relationship.
- I had a lifelong pattern of looking to others to validate me and tell me who I was.
- I hoped that if I could be the person others wanted me to be, then they would love me.
- I was more exhausted than empowered.

I think that most women can relate to this list. In her book *The Confident Woman*, Marjorie Hansen Shaevitz points out a

Female Code of Conduct. I believe it is this kind of conduct code that keeps women fractured and stuck in Surreal Love. She says that no matter what the age, marital status, or ethnic background, what she heard repeatedly from women was:

- The need to be unselfish and nice, and to please everyone but yourself.
- The obsession with looking good rather than treating your body and mind with respect.
- The fear of upsetting or imposing on others, or not meeting some idealized set of behaviors.
- The propensity for being super responsible and trustworthy, except when it comes to yourself.

She says that women feel they must be beautiful, ever youthful, unselfish, responsible, hardworking, ladylike Superwomen. They think they need to be everything to everybody but little or nothing for themselves, and this is when they get into trouble. Being little or nothing for ourselves is what unplugs the power in any empowerment we do have. Remember? We are top priority! Be as beautiful, responsible, and hardworking as you want, not as he wants. When we feel and look beautiful in our own eyes, I promise you, he and the rest of the world will see us as more wonderful than we have ever been. So let's make a choice right now, this very minute. Keep reading and find Real Love for ourselves and our relationship.

BE A "PUTTY-POOPER"

"Man putty" will not work. My man cannot heal me, fill in the wounded parts of me, and/or make me whole. Two halves in a relationship *never* make a whole. It only makes a Surreal relationship. It takes two whole human beings to have a relationship based on Real Love.

To get out of Surreal Love, I had to learn how to stop filling my open wounds with "man putty." This meant knowing how to become a self-validating, authentic, self-confident, self-responsible, whole woman—a woman who has self-wellness. Even though I have never been taught, told, expected, or encouraged to be a whole, self-validating woman, I had the choice. Choosing to become whole is the only choice that matters right now. Once I chose wholeness, the other choices in my life became self-evident.

Identify My Fractures So I Could Heal Them Myself

I had to begin living my life as a self-nourishing, self-validating woman connected with my inner being and inherent worthiness. Fractures are wounds made by external forces such as childhood experiences, prior relationships, etc. We all have them. They may be visible or invisible. As I worked on my internal growth, I learned to see what the "blown-off" pieces of me were. I had to learn the origins of my fractures so that I could begin to heal them now that I was leaving the bondage of Surreal Love.

I began losing my wholeness when just a baby—all of us did. Then, somewhere around the fifth or sixth grade, I gave up more pieces so I could attract boyfriends, belong, and be accepted. I went from being a young girl to being a girlfriend, then a wife, leaving pieces of myself behind in order to fit in. I would have continued this pattern for the rest of my life unless I *stopped*.

5

Save Your Soul by Becoming Whole

SEIZE THE FEELING

In the previous chapter, you uncovered how you lost your "original wholeness" and how this influenced with whom and why you fell in Surreal Love. Discovering what you need to know about yourself in order to begin your journey to wholeness and Real Love is what this chapter is all about. I'm not going to tell you to find your woundedness, recognize old brain messages, heal your fractures with your new brain, and become whole without giving you a guide to accomplish this. I won't leave you stranded. In this chapter, you'll find the first steps to begin emotional healing.

Becoming whole is a huge life-changing event, but it is not nearly as huge as selling out your soul. These are the steps I had to take in order to grow to Real Love. I had to keep them simple for me and I hope this helps you.

After watching the movie *Dead Poet's Society*, I was motivated by a real sense of "carpe diem." You know, seize the day and make every minute count. Accomplish as many projects, meetings, volunteer works, supermom stuff, etc. as you possibly can. Well, it didn't take too long before the carpe diem was giving me a nervous breakdown. That's when my son said I was into "crappy diem" and it was making me "grouchy all the time." How right he was!

I have since learned that the carpe diem vis-à-vis wholeness means "embracing" more than "doing." By that I mean embracing all aspects of life—good and bad. But, most importantly, it means seizing the feeling. By learning how to live life through my heart, I was able to begin moving past existing and into living with Real Love. By staying in "surreal doing mode," I was keeping my feelings at bay. Finding and validating your feelings will lead you to finding your wholeness. As you take the beginning steps to wholeness presented in this chapter, climb each step with passion, compassion, and Real Love for who you were, who you are, and the woman you are becoming.

BEGINNING STEPS TO WHOLENESS MADE SIMPLE

Try to enthusiastically apply these steps as you experience and enjoy each chapter.

1. Be Alive!

Be present. I had to consciously try to not simply go through the motions of living. I would no longer just settle for existence. I tried to understand who I was and where I was in my life. This was no easy task. Here are some questions to ask yourself to help you get started.

How aware are you of your inner world?

You are undoubtedly very aware of your outer world—the world of clothes, furniture, cars, work, appointments, and so on. But how much attention do you give to your inner world and your inner experience? Not only the world of emotions, but your values, feelings, likes, and dislikes? Knowing and acknowledging what is important to you inside is the first step toward wholeness. Begin the search for your soul, mind, and spirit. Listen to your inner voice. It will seem very quiet and hard to hear at first. But by the time you become a "wild woman," you will hear that voice loud and clear. You will know your deepest passion. You will become empowered as you find and nurture your inner world. As you learn to balance your inner experience with your outer world, you will enable yourself to embody your sacredness and your soul.

To begin to become aware of who you are, try the following:

Write five words that describe you right now in this very moment of your life.

1. _____
2. _____
3. _____

4. _____
5. _____

Don't fret or analyze. Simply feel with your heart five words that are descriptions of you. Once you've written them down, leave then alone until we are ready to come back to these words later in the book.

I clearly remember the very first time I wrote down any words that actually described me at a particular point in time. I mean, it had never, ever occurred to me to spend any time at all describing, much less thinking about, who I was. I was way too busy trying to be who I thought I was supposed or expected to be.

I was thirty years old and in law school. One of my professors marched into class and told us that in order to be good lawyers we must learn to be brief and concise in everything we say and do. He then gave us a thirty-second time limit to describe something in five words or less.

In a panic, I described myself:

Happy - Nice - Plain - Sad - Confused

A week later he returned my paper with this note:

Ms. McClary,

I am not sure as to whether I am more disturbed that 1) the something you described was you—or 2) that you do not know the difference between adjectives and your feelings—or 3) that within a thirty-second period of time you could have such conflicting emotions about yourself. I think you should seek professional help.

At the time, I just laughed off his comments. I made an "A" in his class and threw his note in the file cabinet with all my other papers. It stayed there for three years. That's how long it took me to realize that he was one of the wisest professors I had ever known.

Who is running your life right now?

When you give away responsibility for your life—to your man, your parents, media advertising, or whomever—you also give away your power. You become a victim to the whims of others. This suffocates your potential and creativity. How can you possibly feel good about yourself if you let others control your life? This causes you to be and feel subordinate. Victims feel powerless, depressed, and fearful and deny their value. They seek the safety of the familiar and undemanding instead of feeling confident to go after new challenges.

When you take responsibility for your life, you realize how truly powerful you are. You learn how to acknowledge and value your inner authority as a woman. Only then can you begin to experience the creativity, strength, courage, brilliance, and Real Love that come from your core of being. In assuming responsibility for your own life, you trust and, therefore, nourish yourself. Possibly, for the first time, you become the director of your own identity. You finally find and validate your own authority. You give yourself the permission to authorize your *self*. Now your Real Love and creative energy can be reborn and renewed.

Who do you think you are?

Women with high self-esteem attract men with high self-esteem. Most importantly, self-reliant women have a greater chance of forming nourishing relationships, rather than toxic ones. Such a woman will not be devastated by a disappointing relationship, nor will she surrender her life to please a man. Part of having high self-esteem means not being a "Stepford Wife." You know, that movie where the husbands "bump off" their real wives and replace them with look-alike robotic models whom the husbands can program to be the perfect mate. Stepford Wives are physical shells of women with mechanical insides. They do whatever others program them to do.

I am repeatedly disheartened when I see many of my women's health students give up their goals and change their personalities as soon as they meet a man. Like empty-headed "Barbie Dolls," they suddenly develop the same likes and dislikes as their "Ken," wearing the clothes he likes and ignoring their female friends so they can be ready when he calls. I want to pounce on them and yell, "You're not Barbie! Where did the real you go? Come back!" Is this or has this ever been you?

2. Be Honest with Yourself

We women really have trouble being honest with ourselves. So that we won't bother anyone or make anyone uncomfortable, we internalize our dissatisfaction with our lives and our bodies, eventually paying a price for this. For example, for two years I had a big red dot right between my eyebrows. Seriously, I had this bright red rash like a tattoo of the Japanese flag on my forehead. My husband was convinced I had joined a secret religious cult.

Every morning I looked in the mirror and asked myself, "What kind of doctor shall I try this week? Let's see. I've tried two dermatologists already. Maybe I should try an allergist, or how about an internist?" and on and on. I tried every lotion, potion, and over-the-counter or prescription cream available. Nothing worked. This big red dot stared back at me each time I looked at my face (which I did less and less frequently, especially when my five-year-old called me "Rudolph the Head Rose Reindeer" from Thanksgiving until well after Christmas).

Finally one morning I looked at that ridiculous, miraculous, flashing red light between my eyes and actually yelled, "What in the world do you want?!" The red dot yelled back, "I want you to pay attention!" Shocked into silence, I realized it was time for me to practice what I teach.

Be truthful.

First, I started being honest with myself. I had developed many other little ailments over the previous years which had no medical explanations—little nervous twitches, neck pain, too many colds, and so on. I concluded that these physical problems occurred or worsened every time I buried my feelings so my husband, coworkers, and friends would think I was an agreeable and nice person. My honest evaluation of all this resulted in discovering two very important facts: (1) being nice, instead of honest, was my choice, not anyone else's, and (2) being so nice was making me sick.

Pay attention to the truth.

Second, I paid attention to what my body was telling me. To do this, I had to listen and feel with my heart, instead of only with my brain. My heart was hurting and very tired. My feelings told me I did not want to keep my emotions locked up any longer. My health demanded that I express my feelings, whether anger, disagreement, sadness, or mushy love. Memorize this: heart first, head second. Say it over and over, then over and over again.

Apply the wisdom your body and self are teaching you.

I painstakingly acquired the wisdom and respect to listen to my body. Through listening, I did every single thing in this book. I healed me. Healing myself is a continuing and rejuvenating process. Then I began the work of healing the parts of my relationship with my husband that were not honest and authentic. Today, we are doing great and that damn red dot is gone.

When you have a headache or a sick feeling in your stomach, be honest with yourself! Ask the headache or the sick feeling, "What should I be paying attention to?" Then pay attention to your heart's answer. Keep paying attention to your body. Notice where you feel tension. Do your shoulders or neck tighten? Our bodies always give us signals to let us know what is going on. Have the wisdom and respect to listen to your body through your heart. Then you will know with absolute certainty what actions you must take to honor your feelings.

Please set this book down for about one minute. With your heart, not with your eyes, take a good, close look at your wonderful body. What part of you aches? What part of you doesn't feel as well as it could? Write it down. Pay attention. Listen. Fill yourself with your body's wisdom. It will always guide you to what you need to take care of for yourself.

3. Find Yourself—Then Love What You Find

The first and most important relationship you must cherish and honor is with yourself. It is the most intimate relationship and most loving. I know this is a cliché, but it bears repeating because self-loathing is, unfortunately, way too common in women. Only after you learn to love yourself are you capable of truly loving another. Your body will never feel like home to you if you are not comfortable with and accepting of who you really are. Once you care for yourself, you can care for someone else.

Put yourself first.

Make lists of the things you like to do, the places you like to go, and the people you truly enjoy—going way back into your childhood. Recall as vividly as possible what it felt like to do and be in those activities and places and with those people. How did you feel? You probably felt alive, happy, balanced, accepted, and loved. Even though you may attribute your feelings to the circumstances or people, you were really experiencing what it is like to be yourself.

A surreal woman tends to make everyone else's needs a priority and ignore her own. If this is you, try doing the "Priority Challenge."

Make a list of the things you do well and those you would love to learn how to do. Don't think about how impractical they seem, or how inconsequential, or whether someone might say they are crazy. Your self-esteem will soar as you explore the talents, interests, passions, and gifts that you have been given, not those others think you should develop. We will come back to these in the next section. This is very important for Real Love.

Here is a sample of what my list looked like:

Things I Do Well

Intellectual	Creative	Relationships	Self
• *teach*	• *music*	• *love my children*	• *walks*
• *read*	• *books*	• *love my family*	• *movies*
• *write articles*		• *love hubby best I can*	• *sleep late*
		• *love my friends and students*	• *margaritas on the beach*

Things I Would Like to Learn How to Do

Intellectual	Creative	Relationships	Self
• *understand weird stuff (like cosmos and energy fields and auras)*	• *play bass guitar*	• *same as above*	• *dance*
	• *sing*		• *let loose*
	• *play piano*		• *be wild & crazy (sometimes)*
• *figure out the universe*	• *be a rock star*		

Challenge yourself to write down five things you enjoy and are willing to make a priority in your life. Things that will help you find yourself, be yourself, and enjoy yourself. Examples of some of my priorities were to read more books, go to the movies, make appointments for annual check-ups, and to go on more walks. Be specific. Don't just write "be a better mom" or "have more time for myself."

Once you have listed five priorities, keep a "time diary" for two days (forty-eight hours). This is simply a diary of how you actually spend your time. To do this, make three columns on a piece of paper. There's no need to get fancy here. I just slapped my columns down on a paper napkin, threw it in my purse, and scribbled notes all over it for two days. Label your columns as:

Time	_Occurrence_	_Thoughts_

Under "Time," put a time span, such as 8:00 a.m. to 9:00 a.m. Under "Occurrence," jot down what you did during this time. Under "Thoughts," write what your thoughts are at regarding how you spent this time. You may want to do the "Thoughts" column in the evenings when you can get a few minutes to yourself. If possible, do them right after you jot down occurrences. Here's how one of my first diaries began:

Time	_Occurrence_	_Thoughts_
7–8 a.m.	got dressed, got kids dressed, fixed breakfast, got kids to school and me to work	I'm frazzled already and the day has just begun!
8–9 a.m.	studied notes for classes	I can't keep my eyes open. I'm so sleepy.

After two days, review your diary and see how much, if any, of your time was devoted to your priorities. I was shocked to see that not one minute of the two-day period was spent on any of the priorities I listed. But when I thought about it, I immediately realized why. When it came to myself, I would always plan on getting to what I needed "later." Unfortunately, later usually meant never. But it took a napkin diary to wake me up and really make me see this.

I decided to start small with little changes that would make a big difference. I made sure I allowed at least fifteen minutes for myself at least four times a day. For example, from 8:45 to 9:00 a.m., I took a short walk instead of staying at my desk. No phone call, email, student, or fear of being unprepared for class could keep me from my walk. I was amazed how much more focused, revived, alert, and awake these walks made me feel. At 3:45 p.m. every afternoon, I would take at least ten minutes to plan for what I needed. This was the most productive ten minutes of the entire day as far as my priorities were concerned. I not only scheduled previously delayed healthcare appointments, but I also made the arrangements with hubby or a baby-sitter so that I had time for a movie, book club, dance lesson, or just a few hours to myself. Now, whenever I feel I am losing sight of my priorities, I do a quick one- or two-day diary on whatever is handy (paper towel, lunch bag, or grocery store receipt) and set myself on the right track again.

Make a note of each time you feel tempted to do something you know in your heart you do not want to do. Especially make note if you are worried that if you don't do it you might not be accepted by a man (or even your friends). Stop! Ask yourself, "Is this a pattern?" We all must compromise now and then, and it's fun to try new things and accept new challenges. But to accept yourself, you must be willing to put your Self first and know yourself well enough to know whether or not you truly want to do what you are being asked. The Dalai Lama summed it up well by reminding us to always follow the three R's:

Respect for self
Respect for others
Responsibility for all your actions

I had to work very hard at putting myself first. My mantra became, "How do I love me? Let me count the ways." As a young girl, I loved dancing, reading books, taking long walks, and team sports. I discovered that I missed these things. I also missed spending time with girlfriends. I started immediately. I joined a contra dancing group, signed up for piano lessons, and took long walks by myself after dinner. I built and strengthened my friendships and, therefore, my network of support. How mistaken I had been to believe one person could meet all my needs—especially since that person was a clueless man! I was, still am, and always will have a wonderful time being with me.

Accept your body.

Many women have poor body image. Well, no wonder. If high heels were so great, men would still be wearing them! Everywhere we look, we take the heat for looking "abnormal" as judged by the standards of the media, magazine ads, movies, televisions, billboards—it's everywhere! It is so surreal! Who is this airbrushed, pore-free, nonwrinkled, painfully thin, flawless woman? She makes me so angry! I know I never will see her, yet she assaults me on a daily basis.

Whose standard of beauty do you measure yourself by—daVinci, Andy Warhol, *Teen* magazine?

Did you know:

- If shop mannequins were live women, they'd be too thin to menstruate?
- There are three billion women who do not look like super models and only eight who do.
- Marilyn Monroe wore a size fourteen.
- If Barbie were a real woman, she'd have to walk on all fours due to her proportions.
- The average woman weighs 144 pounds and wears between a size twelve and fourteen.
- One out of every four college-age women has an eating disorder.

- The photos of the models in the magazines are airbrushed.
- A psychological study in 1995 found that three minutes spent looking at models in a fashion magazine caused 70 percent of women to feel depressed, guilty, and ashamed.
- Twenty years ago, models weighed 8 percent less than the average women. Today, models weigh 23 percent less.

We women should be proud, no matter what our size. There is absolutely no fashion faux pas we could make that could ever rival the Speedo—*eeech*.

Strut your stuff.

Do something, large or small, that makes you feel great about you. Walk three times a week. Jog in front of the television. I like to pretend to jog right into George Clooney's blue eyes. Change your hair color. Wear what makes you feel good. Yes, even though *he* might not like it. Erase the negative messages you play in your brain every time you look in the mirror. Replace them with positive ones. Just as astronomers do for planets, we should name our stretch marks after great composers, authors, and artists. I've named mine alphabetically, and I'm up to Renoir.

I relish the fact that no matter where I live I am a true Southern Belle: With each passing year another part of my body heads directly south. When I look in the mirror, I turn off the negative tapes of aging, more wrinkles, and sags. Instead, my brain immediately clicks into a beautiful tape of freedom, power, and sensuality that instantly makes me feel good about myself.

However, the most rewarding thing I do when I start to worry about getting older is just pull out my old high school yearbook and take a look. Aaagh! I look like a corpse with braces and zits! Suddenly (once I stop laughing), I become very grateful that I have aged. And if I really need an age-related pick-me-up, I just go have breakfast at McDonald's. All those nice old guys in there think they've died and gone to heaven when some fifty-year-old spring chicken comes prancing in. They tip their hats, nod at you, smile, and make you feel gorgeous. Thank you, "Egg McMuffin Men!" I love ya!

From now on, when someone gives you a compliment, respond with a thank you and an embellishment. Never again give a negative response to positive verbal gifts. For example, in the past when someone would say something nice about me, such as "Cheryl, that's a very pretty dress on you," I could not accept it. I would immediately negate and invalidate the compliment by saying something like, "This old thing?" or "Oh thanks, but after lunch there's no way it will still fit." I was sabotaging myself, the compliment, and the person who said something nice.

I eventually made myself learn to say thank you and then learn to be quiet. Someone would compliment me, I would thank them, and I would not say anything else that might undermine things. When I became very comfortable with the simple "thank you," I moved to the next step. Now when someone delivers a compliment, I thank them and add on to the positive vibes. If someone is kind enough to say they like my dress, I say, "Thank you! I love it too! It's one of my very favorite things to wear!" I affirm me and the other person. Does that ever feel good!

Maybe this email I received one day will help you put "strutting your stuff" in perspective.

Age 8: A young girl looks at herself and sees a lovely Cinderella or Sleeping Beauty.

Age 15: A young woman looks at herself and sees Cinderella, Sleeping Beauty, or maybe a Cheerleader. But if she is PMS-ing she sees a fat, pimpled, UGLY person and yells, "Mom, I can't go to school looking like this!"

Age 20: A young woman looks at herself and sees a person who is too fat/too thin, too short/too tall, too straight/too curly—but decides she's going anyway.

Age 30: She looks at herself and sees a person who is too fat/too thin, too short/too tall, too straight/too curly—but decides she doesn't have time to fix it, so she's going anyway.

Age 40: She looks at herself and sees a person who is too fat/too thin, too short/too tall, too straight/too curly—but says, "At least I'm clean" and goes anyway.

Age 50: She looks at herself and says, "I am" and goes wherever she wants to.

Age 60: She looks at herself and reminds herself of all the people who can't even see themselves in the mirror anymore. Goes out and conquers the world.

Age 70: She looks at herself and sees wisdom, laughter, and ability, and goes out and enjoys life.

Age 80: She doesn't bother to look. Just puts on a red hat and goes out to participate in the world.

4. Affirm Yourself

Once you begin loving yourself and expressing the self you love, others will take notice. Fears about losing friends and family when we change are usually unfounded. Although some people may have trouble accepting this new assertive and affirmative you, decide that any person who does not accept you as you are is not someone you wish to be with. By being who you are, you will attract people who love you for this very quality! After all, we can only expect others to respect us if we respect ourselves first.

Make a quick list right now. On the left side, list your "Positive Friends." These are people who love the real you. These are the friends and family members that you know in your heart want you to be yourself around them. They may even give you a hard time when you try to be someone you're not.

On the right side, list your "Negative Friends." These are the friends and relatives who only like you when you behave the way they expect or want you to behave. You know exactly who I am talking about because it doesn't feel very good to think about them.

Now look hard at your list. Treasure, nurture, and cultivate the positive relationships in your life. These feed your soul. Eliminate or give as little time as possible to your negative relationships. These people wear you down and make you tired.

Walk forward, not backward.

When in relationships with men, work hard to maintain your sense of self. It is very easy to slide back into old habits. Men can often be very good at provoking your deepest self-doubts. Some will even try to sabotage you into returning to your old ways. Men often do this when they are feeling insecure and need to boost their own egos. But let's face it—men feel much less guilty when it comes to work and relationships. How many times have you heard a man ask advice on how to combine marriage and a career?

Self-doubt is the enemy of self-acceptance. When you feel self-doubt creeping in, call up a vivid image of a time when you felt powerful and whole. Affirm for yourself: I am whole, I love myself, I am powerful, and nobody can take my power from me without my permission. You do not need others to validate who you are. Reminding yourself of this requires constant vigilance. Sometimes it seems as if there is always someone in your life who makes you try to doubt yourself. When you are able to hold back the rising tide of your self-doubt, you know your self-esteem is on the mend.

Use as Needed When Someone Has Caused Self-Doubt to Creep In:

Dear Boyfriend, Date, Lover, etc.,

What I love best about myself is that I can fall head-over-heels, madly in love with you, and if you don't call back or aren't around the next day, I know it is your loss.

I had a great time being in love with you. I hope you have the courage to someday work through everything that scares you about loving a wonderful, wild woman like me.

Dear Partner, Husband, etc.,

What I love best about myself is that every day I fall "head-over-heels," crazy in love with you all over again. And even if you try to shut me out, ignore me, or withdraw from me, I know it is your loss.

I have such a great time loving you. My wish for you is that someday you will have the courage and strength to work through all the things that scare you about loving a beautiful, wonderfully wild woman like me. How incredible it would be if we could go through life embracing our love for each other.

Dear Dad, Mom, Grandmom, etc.,

What I love best about you being my Dad (or Mom, etc.) is that you have helped me have the strength and courage never to doubt myself when I absolutely know in my heart that I am right (or doing the right thing).

No matter how much you criticize me or disagree with me or my life, I still love you and always will. I feel so blessed to be your daughter.

Dear Whoever Is Giving You a Hard Time and You're Too Tired to Deal With It,

   Hand over the chocolate and nobody gets hurt.

Be assertive

Being assertive means being willing to protect your right to be whole by being strong enough to seek and find the lost pieces of your soul. Being whole does not mean being perfect. Wholeness means knowing who you are and where you end and others begin. This is called having boundaries. As you become empowered, you learn not only how to make boundaries, but also how to protect them. When I was in surrealness, I wouldn't have even dreamed of telling my kids and husband to take care of themselves for an hour while I practiced the piano. Now that I'm empowered towards Real Love, I don't hesitate to tell my family that no one is to disturb me for one hour (sometimes one day) while I'm playing music. Creating music is one of my sacred boundaries. Locking the door to the den and making my man be responsible for running the household for a while ensures that my boundary is protected and not inappropriately or inconsiderately crossed.

Know your boundaries

The person that has helped me the most to understand my right to develop, know, and enforce my boundaries is my sons' martial arts instructor.

Carl Wilcox states that there are four types of boundaries that human beings should have in order to be empowered: physical, sexual, emotional, and spiritual. To begin to understand and know your own boundaries, make the following position statements right now:

Physical boundaries: I have the right to determine when, where, how, and who is going to touch me. I have the right to determine how close someone is going to stand next to me.

Sexual boundaries: I have the right to determine with whom, where, when, and how I am going to be sexual.

Emotional boundaries: What I think and feel, do or don't do is more about me than it is about you. Conversely, what you think and feel, do or don't do is more about you than it is about me.

Spiritual boundaries: I have the right to think and believe as I do. I need face only the consequences of my own thinking.

Boundaries may be visualized as a malleable plastic bubble that exists around a person. It is flexible and permeable. For instance, if I choose to hug someone, I choose to allow them into my physical boundary, just as they choose to let me into theirs. If I choose to be sexual with someone, I choose to let them into my physical and sexual boundaries. If I choose to share my deepest feelings, I allow a person to enter my emotional boundary.

Allowing a person access to us, inside our boundaries, is a gesture of trust and intimacy. We make ourselves vulnerable. We can either experience affirmation or be wounded to the core. Boundaries offer protection from the emotional and physical assaults of others.

Healthy boundaries, though not perfect, are made by our rational new brain. They allow a person to experience a comfortable interdependence with other people, resulting in emotionally healthy relationships and wholeness.

Damaged boundaries operate inconsistently out of old-brain functioning. They are the result of mixed messages and dysfunction. They are usually related to unresolved, unhealthy relationships in the individual's family of origin and/or relationships of choice.

Boundaries are not walls. Walls protect the person who has constructed them but do not let anything in or out. This person lives in a state of loneliness, possibly protected from the assaults of others but also prevented from establishing trusting and intimate relationships. People with walled boundaries have generally been deeply hurt by others. They have erected barriers to prevent being hurt again by others' actions, thoughts, and feelings instead of working on self-wellness.

Signs of Healthy Boundaries

- Appropriate trust
- Revealing a little of yourself at a time, then checking to see how the other person responds to you sharing
- Moving step-by-step into intimacy
- Putting a new acquaintanceship on hold until you check for compatibility
- Deciding whether a potential relationship will be good for you
- Staying focused on your own growth and recovery
- Weighing the consequence before acting on sexual impulse
- Being sexual when you want to be sexual—concentrating largely on your own pleasure rather than monitoring the reactions of your partner
- Maintaining personal values despite what others want
- Noticing when someone else displays inappropriate

boundaries

- Noticing when someone invades your boundaries
- Saying "no" to food, gifts, touches, sex you don't want
- Asking a person before touching them
- Respect for others—not taking advantage of someone's generosity
- Self-respect—not giving too much in the hope that someone will like you
- Not allowing someone to take advantage of your generosity
- Trusting your own decisions
- Defining your truth, as you see it
- Knowing who you are and what you want
- Recognizing that friends and partners are not mind-readers
- Clearly communicating your wants and needs (and recognizing that you may be turned down, but you can ask)
- Becoming your own loving parent
- Talking to yourself with gentleness, humor, love, and respect

Wholeness is expressed as the ability to listen to and communicate your honest feelings. Only after eighteen years of marriage did I finally break down enough internal walls to free my true and authentic feelings. By relating to my husband through my honest feelings, I have discovered the emotional strength to successfully stop him from going alien on me.

Being assertive and having boundaries also means noticing in what situations or with which people you feel unlovable. Stop! Do not give your power away! Do not let a man (or anyone else) keep you from being who you want to be. Love is the heartfelt desire to support another person in being all he or she can be. It is not about making that person into your image of who you want. Just like he should not want you to be a Stepford wife, you should not want him to be Tom Hanks. You are not trying to change him into someone else, you are trying to find him: the real, authentic human being deep inside. It is too hard to stay in love for the long haul with a man who is not real. If you love him, you will not allow him to control you because that does not support him in becoming the true human being he can be. If he loves you, he will rejoice in your feeling good about yourself.

You cannot seek love of self through love of another. Your love of yourself cannot be defined by what he does or does not do.

5. Belief in Yourself

One of the goals for Real Love is to learn to act out of choice rather than acting to gain acceptance, approval, or to feel needed. To feel free to choose, you must believe in yourself. When you know who you are and what you believe, you will feel free to establish boundaries between yourself and others.

You must know the answer to these questions before you will ever know when and if your boundaries have ever been crossed.

What in life is really important to you?

What you know, I mean really know, never changes. This knowledge comes from your heart, not your head. You are not obligated to prove it to anyone. You must know what you want in order to ask for it. Develop a clear sense of your values. Define and redefine your boundaries, being clear about what is and is not acceptable behavior from others. In other words, value your own knowing. It will always guide you to what is best for you.

What do you hold sacred?

Sacred means "entitled to reverence" and "inviolable." What you hold sacred may include your religion or views on God, but it can also include your moral beliefs, your philosophy of life, your deepest connections to the universe, your family, your community, and friends. Clarify and write down your ethics. Search deep within and ask yourself what is sacred to you. Is there anything that is so important and meaningful that you would be willing to give your life for it? Feel with all your heart and know absolutely these answers.

Now with total conviction, write it down.

~:~

"I, _____ (name), hold the following things sacred:

   1. _____

   2. _____

   3. _____

   4. (or more) _____

"I will never allow anyone to violate what is sacred to me."

_____   _____

          Signed   Date

~:~

Renew your sacred connections daily. Celebrate your uniqueness and your wholeness. Trust yourself and your intuition. Feel the spirit and energy that can be gained by living intentionally, fully, and with passion.

There is even more good news. As you leave Surreal Love and become more whole and in Real Love, you will become less depressed. I am referring to the "run-of-the-mill, down-in-the dumps" kind of mild depression affecting one in ten women at any given time. Clinical depression, the "you-cannot-get-out-of-bed or make-a-cup-of-coffee" kind of major depression is a whole other matter for which you should seek help.

Signs of major depression could be significant weight loss or gain, turning to alcohol or other drugs, feeling hopeless or worthless, feeling overwhelmed by sadness or of "going crazy," frightening physical symptoms, and/or thoughts of death or suicide. Call a professional counselor if you are feeling these kinds of symptoms.

In the next chapter, I will help you to find ways to feel less stressed, depressed, and anxious. It is so easy for us to get overwhelmed and lose sight of our true journey. I want to show you ways to get more "underwhelmed" and have some fun de-stressing on the way to wholeness.

6

*Don't Worry—"Stressed" Is "Desserts"
Spelled Backwards*

KEEP THE PACE, NOT THE PEACE

Women get depressed when they aren't, or feel they can't be, whole. And when you are not whole you are not your true self. This means your life feels unpredictable and uncontrollable—the main causes of depression in women. As you journey towards Real Love and gain predictability and control in your relationship and your life, you *will* feel better.

It is hard for a woman to establish and maintain personal relationships while preserving her inner or true self. In Surreal women the inner self is "silenced" for the sake of keeping the relationship. To silence your inner self you are forced to give up control—control of your conversation, control of your inner needs, control over how you feel, and control over who you are. When this happens, you have automatically lost predictability because you have no way of knowing how or why or what you are going to say or do at any given time. When women silence their inner selves, the high price they pay for keeping peace in their relationships is depression and/or anxiety. Relationships should not be a source of depression or anxiety. When you are whole, relationships become a path to finding meaning in your life.

Anxiety is continuous worry. It is constant buzzing of worrisome thoughts you cannot turn off. Like depression, anxiety can be chronic and require professional treatment if it interferes with daily activities and is accompanied by various physical symptoms such as shortness of breath, dizziness, and heart palpitations. No one's life is a smooth, even line of serenity. When you are depressed or anxious, it is important to pace yourself and stay calm while you continue to strengthen and nurture your inner self so you will have the energy necessary to find your answers.

Here are some ways to nurture yourself if you get depressed or anxious, or just need to be good to yourself:

CHOCOLATE IS GOOD FOR YOU AND A BALANCED DIET IS A COOKIE IN EACH HAND

Engage in a timed crying session, but do not get lost in it. Once your time is up (fifteen to forty-five minutes), watch a funny movie, read an uplifting book, go to the mall, or attend an exciting sports event to energize your spirits. I have grown to love hockey games (Go Asheville Smoke!). What a trip! I get to scream, yell, shake my fists, and act totally out of control. Even though my kids won't sit in the same row with me, I leave the games exhausted and exhilarated. It's a surefire depression lifter every time. Treating yourself to some sensory pleasures such as chocolate, a glass of wine, a make-up makeover, or even a pair of earrings may help.

Have some fun and get a temporary tattoo painted on. Moderation is the key. If you eat, drink, spend too much money, or watch too much television, you will become more depressed or anxious. Be gentle with yourself. Think about treating yourself with a pedicure, a bikini wax, or a massage—anything you do not normally do for yourself.

And I'm serious about this chocolate issue. As far as I'm concerned, chocolate covered raisins, cherries, orange slices, and strawberries all count as a fruit serving. Eat as many as you want. I always put "eat chocolate" at the top of my "to do" list for the day. That way, I know I'll get at least one thing done. And have you noticed that there is no such organization as Chocoholics Anonymous? No one wants to quit! In summary, in my life, money talks, but chocolate sings! I just go ahead and accept that if I am what I eat, then I'm either fast, cheap, or easy! Deal with it!

Exercise

To get out of a depression you need to move from your low arousal state into high arousal, through something like aerobic exercise. Running, team sports, dancing, and sex are forms of aerobics. Aerobic exercise lifts mild depression and can dissipate a bad mood, especially for people who are not exercise addicts.

If you experience anxiety rather than depression, however, you are in a very high arousal state. You need activities that will lower your arousal level such as yoga, meditation, massage, tai chi, or a hot bath, preferably accompanied by soothing music and surrounded by candles.

If you are depressed and anxious, go for a walk. There is nothing better than a nice walk to help clear your head so you can feel with your heart. A refreshing walk will always help you regain your perspective and may even turn anxiety into inspiration! (Particularly if you walk to the nearest Red Lobster and have cheese biscuits and margaritas!)

Engage in a purposeful task

Tackle some long-delayed chore like clearing your closet of old clothes, shaving your legs, returning phone calls. The goal here is to engineer some small triumph or easy success. Try a new recipe or bake one of your old favorites. Sew, draw, paint, or make a collage from old magazine pictures. Clean out your car, then give it a wash and wax. The list is limited only by your imagination, lifestyle, and abilities.

My family is still laughing at the above paragraph. Okay. I admit it. Whenever I feel the urge to clean, I lie down and get over it. I am no Martha Stewart. The thought of watching her show gives me hives. Making a lampshade cover is way too hard for me. My "purposeful task" must always be very simple. Therefore, I organize with a capital "O"!

I often get depressed when I am completely overwhelmed and my life seems totally chaotic. Organizing anything always makes me feel better. Sometimes I take all of two minutes to sit on the floor of the closet and separate my black shoes from the cream-colored ones (the only two colors I have). Then I stand up and congratulate myself on how organized I am. This vision of my organized shoes keeps my spirits lifted for days.

When my life is really out of control (you know, those days you keep checking to see if you are "buttoned" and "zippered" because you have no memory of whether or not you put on your clothes that morning), my organizing must take on bolder proportions. Sometimes I organize a bathroom cabinet, the pantry, maybe even a photograph album. I can always count on purposeful organizing to make me feel better, and believe that at least something is organized in my life.

Look at the situation differently

Cognitive reframing means looking at something in a different light, like having great body image as long as you don't weigh more than the refrigerator. This helps you put things in perspective. Make a list of all the good things in your life like margaritas, chocolate, your best friend from high school, a car that runs, and so on. Realize that a clean house is the sign of a misspent life. Recognize that a balanced diet can be a salad, a diet Coke, and a hot fudge sundae. And, of course, trust in the inaccuracy of every bathroom scale ever made. After all, if stress burned calories, we would all be a size zero. Make a list of all your successes, no matter how small. Keep a gratitude journal and at the end of each day write down what you have to be grateful for. If you don't have time to write it down, just take a few minutes when you can't sleep at night and think about the things that make you feel blessed.

Help others

Send a note or call all the women you are grateful to have as friends. Visit people at the hospital, or give time to premature babies who need someone to rock them. Sing for the elderly. Stock shelves at the food bank. Deliver Meals on Wheels. Tutor a child. Your local United Way or Chamber of Commerce can direct you to the right place. Just do something for others, for people in need—really in need, not simply a friend who needs help polishing off a box of Girl Scout Cookies before they spoil.

Turn to a higher power

Whatever your belief system, use it. Spiritual prayer has been proven to work and the power of prayer has saved many a woman. The spirit of a woman is her interior essence that responds to the preciousness of life and to the beautiful uniqueness of ourselves and others. Cultivate, treasure, and nurture your spirit. This will always help you awaken to a sense of purpose and joy of life that cannot only sustain you through the tough times but, more importantly, can profoundly enrich your life celebrations. Keep in mind that sorrow looks backward and worry looks forward. But, somehow, faith and spirit always look up.

Laugh

Humor cuts through anxiety by creating endorphin highs that lift the heart. In painful or fearful situations, humor provides a chance to recharge and refresh. When you engage your sense of humor, you become more compassionate and forgiving, and it becomes easier to accept yourself and others. Research shows that laughing can help you think more broadly and associate more freely as well as help you find a creative solution to a problem. Laughter enhances the immune system and reduces physical as well as emotional tension. There's nothing like a good laugh to help you get in a better mood.

By the way, did you hear the one about the guy who wanted the perfect tan? There was this guy who wanted his body to be perfectly tanned all over. After lying on the beach all day, he went home, took a shower, then looked in the mirror. Aagh! His body was beautifully bronzed except for his ghostly white penis! So first thing the next morning he ran back out to the beach. He covered his entire body under sand, but left his penis out to bake in the sun.

Along came Myrtle and Lucy, two ladies in their seventies, out for their early morning walk.

Myrtle stares ahead at the sand. She can't believe her eyes! She quickly elbows Lucy and says, "Lucy, take a look at that! You know, Lucy…

when I was in my teens—I was ignorant of it

when I was in my 20's—I was scared of it

when I was in my 30's—I liked it

when I was in my 40's—I loved it

when I was in my 50's—I paid for it
when I was in my 60's—I prayed for it
now here I am in my 70's—and the damn things are growin' wild!"

Feel safe

Know that whatever comes your way in life, you will adapt, survive, and transcend. When I have trouble feeling safe in today's crazy world, I check into a hotel room for a night. It doesn't matter if it is a Motel 8 or the Hilton. You just can't beat having a night to yourself, safely tucked in a room with a TV, soft bed, and a mini-bar.

Quiet your mind

Most of us are overwhelmed. Please give yourself fifteen to twenty minutes a day for quiet time. Spend the time in meditation, walking along a path, or lying quietly on a sofa with no distractions. Breathe, relax, and let go of all responsibility. Do not feel guilty! I know, I know—the house is a wreck, or you have an exam to study for, or your two-year-old's diaper is bigger than he is. Believe me, you will accomplish the millions of things that will still be waiting there for you to do. But you will be in a much better frame of mind if you will take these few minutes to ground yourself.

Quite frankly, I don't really know how to meditate, do yoga, go into a trance, or any of that kind of stuff. I wish I did, but I haven't taken the time to learn. For those of you in the same situation, here's a few tips on how to relax:

Five-Minute Relaxation
1. Get comfortable
2. Close your eyes
3. Slowly breathe in through your nose to the count of four
4. Slowly breathe out through your mouth to the count of four
5. Block out any other thoughts, no matter how important they may seem
6. Continue for five to ten minutes if possible. (If not, just do it for even two or three minutes and you'll feel better.)

Ask for support

If you listen to yourself and your body, you will know if you need to find a support person. This may be a trained counselor or a wise friend. Most importantly, this person needs to be someone who believes in you and your ability to find the answers for yourself. Someone who can support and guide you without imposing their views on you. Sometimes it takes a bit of searching to find the right person, but the main thing is to do it if you need it. There is great strength in asking for help when needed, rather than denying a problem exists.

Choose the journey to wholeness, the path to self-confidence and Real Love. Learn to never again sacrifice yourself for a man or anyone else who believes you should be someone other than who you are. If you continue to keep losing yourself, the relationship is lost anyway. You truly are the strong one now. You are in control of the exciting changes about to occur because you are no longer in denial and have decided to be real. Keep things in perspective. Let go of trying to figure him out. Remind yourself that the man you love is not impossible. He's just clueless. Women who continue to follow their path towards healing and wholeness will find resources they never dreamed of within themselves. And believe me, bringing Real Love into your relationship is going to take resources you have never dreamed of. You're gonna love it!

{SECTION III}

The Outpatient Recovery Guide for Women

7

Learn From the Mistakes of Others—You Can't Make Them All Yourself

WOMAN NARROWLY PASSES LIFE'S MULTIPLE-CHOICE EXAM

This is my life. I have three choices.

A. I can choose not to face my fears and continue to live unconsciously. If I am unwilling to feel fear, I will carry it around forever. I will keep making sure that everyone around me feels great because this will keep me from having to feel my own feelings. With this choice, I live only half a life at the most—and half-lives decay at a predetermined rate, slowly eliminating my true self.

B. I can choose to live in a perpetual state of fear, anger, and/or unhappiness. This choice is even more destructive than a half-life. When I live through fear and anger, I have nothing. When I live through fear eventually I get what I fear. For example, if I am afraid my partner will leave me, I will at some point lose this partner, emotionally, physically, or completely.

C. I can choose to live wholly, to be! I can make it my priority to face my fears; deal with my anger, pain, and hurt; honestly communicate with the one I love; and be willing to deal openly with any consequences. I can experience each emotion as an empowerment and expansion into enthusiasm. This choice will yield the most incredible rewards and be the most freeing experience I will ever have. There is no greater feeling than loving myself as I am, because that love casts out all fear. Most importantly, I can then live my life with passion, enthusiasm, and Real Love. I can be—be who I am and love myself for it! The moment I touch my life with Real Love, I heal. Fear begins to disappear.

To Be or Not To Be—It's Not a Question!

As you can imagine, simply joining the Army won't make you "Be All You Can Be." But once you've made the choice to be whole, you will do the work it takes. Your soul will always show you the way. One day I was "swimming" in the ocean and I heard my soul, I mean really heard it, for the first time. My soul said, "Cheryl—Every day you are alive is a special occasion. Every minute is a gift from God. Don't put off, hold back, or save for later anything that would add laughter and luster to your life.

See, hear, and do it now. Dance like nobody's watching and love like it's never going to hurt. Life is a journey to savor, not endure. Now get with the game plan!" Then a big wave came and hit me so hard it knocked my drink out of my hand and turned my inner tube over. Okay, okay—I get the message!

I know what you are probably thinking (or screaming) about now, and I agree. You are getting fed up with all the talk shows and books always telling you that the reason you are sad or depressed is because you are not whole enough, grateful enough, thankful enough, spirited enough, and on and on. And you're saying, "But I am thankful, I am spiritual, I am trying to find wholeness—and I still feel like I've been ridden hard and worn out!"

Just like everything else you know is important to your health, things are always easier said than done. It's easy to say you should exercise more, lose weight, quit smoking, or become whole. But, you must want to do it and you must be given the information regarding how to do it for a permanent life-giving change to occur. You can't just keep hoping change will happen. You have to make it happen!

Take a second, feel with your heart, and say, "I want to begin the journey to wholeness." Done! You've taken the first step.

It would be wonderful if you could read all the hundreds of great books on wholeness, soulfulness, and finding yourself. (I list some of them for you in the Resource section.) But, if you are like most women, you don't have time to go buy the books much less find time to read them. What follows is the information you need to understand about what wholeness is and how to achieve self-wellness in your life.

This Way to the Wholeness Shelter

At some point in your childhood, you learned to go unconscious in order to survive. You buried your own needs and your sense of self deep inside and learned to over-accommodate others as a way to feel good about yourself. As you have aged and experienced things, you have begun to question your attitudes (or you would not be reading this book). To heal, you must learn that love starts with oneself and moves outward. Healing means becoming whole and involves passing through a continuum of stages marked by salient emotions. Each stage is a passage, not an end. All emotions have a healing purpose. As you grow emotionally and come closer to the healing level of "Real Love," the more motivated you will be to feel and become whole! In other words, you have to know at what emotional level you are living your life right now. Once you recognize the level, only then can you begin to see what changes you can make to begin living in an emotionally better place, the place of Real Love. You have to get to the emotional healing level of Real Love before you can see what's inside you and begin to feel Real Love and thankfulness. Only after you become more whole will you begin to hold your mate more accountable as a human being and a partner.

To understand where you are, look at the following stages of emotional growth leading to wholeness and examine how you are living your life. Later in this book, I will take you through my personal journey through the stages of emotional growth.

Climbing the Ladder to Real Love

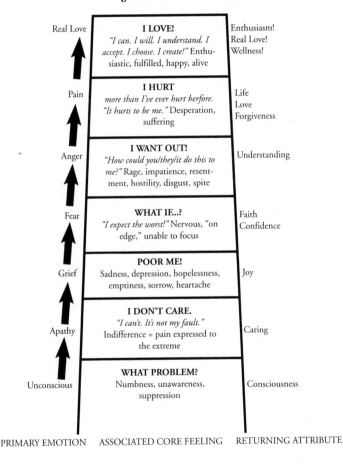

PRIMARY EMOTION	ASSOCIATED CORE FEELING	RETURNING ATTRIBUTE
Real Love	**I LOVE!** *"I can. I will. I understand. I accept. I choose. I create!"* Enthusiastic, fulfilled, happy, alive	Enthusiasm! Real Love! Wellness!
Pain	**I HURT** *more than I've ever hurt berfore.* *"It hurts to be me."* Desperation, suffering	Life Love Forgiveness
Anger	**I WANT OUT!** *"How could you/they/it do this to me?"* Rage, impatience, resentment, hostility, disgust, spite	Understanding
Fear	**WHAT IF...?** *"I expect the worst!"* Nervous, "on edge," unable to focus	Faith Confidence
Grief	**POOR ME!** Sadness, depression, hopelessness, emptiness, sorrow, heartache	Joy
Apathy	**I DON'T CARE.** *"I can't. It's not my fault."* Indifference = pain expressed to the extreme	Caring
Unconscious	**WHAT PROBLEM?** Numbness, unawareness, suppression	Consciousness

*The information regarding stages of emotional healing was compiled from many different sources from Freud to Elizabeth Kübler-Ross. But I give most of the credit to Robert Tennyson Stevens because in his "Mastery of Emotions" tape he conveyed the message in a way that could be understood.

Each emotion has purpose. Some wonderful, amazing attribute always returns when an emotion is fully experienced. Feeling an emotion will bring acceptance and understanding. This will lead to forgiveness and love. As you feel your emotions you will begin to feel your health return. As this happens, you begin gently guiding yourself towards the wholeness of Real Love.

Examining each level separately makes the continuum easier to understand, but most of us experience a shifting up and down between levels within days, minutes, or seconds. Even when living life through the emotion of Real Love, there will be times when life events cause feelings of anger, pain, or grief. Once you have attained the level of Real Love, however, you can respond to these feelings from your love rather than getting lost in the emotions. So what does it take to get there?

Realize that what we feel is what we have in our life. We must feel something other than resistance to who we really are. We began life as fully conscious, enthusiastic, feeling human beings. Then many different things chipped away at us, often to the point where we quit feeling.

But we can no longer blame anyone but ourselves for our present state of emotional well-being. We can make the difference in our lives by owning our feelings. We can make the choice to get our feelings and emotions back and become whole again. We must be personally responsible for the return of our emotions. If we continue to suppress them, we are going against the law of love.

Once You Quit Resisting, You Get Something Amazing in Return!

Once you quit resisting your emotions, they will no longer be suppressed. It takes an incredible amount of energy to keep your emotions suppressed. It is exhausting! Feel your emotions with love for yourself and tell yourself it's okay! For example, when you are fully experiencing anger, be very gentle with yourself. Treat yourself as if you are a small child you are angry with. Many times a day tell yourself the following: "I love me. It is okay to love me. It's always best to act out of love for myself."

Unfortunately, most of us were taught not to express or even feel our emotions. How many times have you been told, "You shouldn't feel that way." We constantly resist our emotions so that we stay in control, don't embarrass anybody, and don't look foolish. Doing this has caused a huge problem because what you resist is what you take on!

If you say it is okay for you to fear, you will no longer be afraid. If you say it is okay for you to be angry, you will no longer be angry. It is only "resistance" that is keeping us from being ourselves. Quit resisting and let it be all right that an emotion is there. Quit spending your energy trying to resist who he is, and just be who you are. This is what loving yourself is all about. Never ask how to love, just do it! This is your power! You win!

Moving out of unconsciousness takes responding to a wake-up call. This simply means saying you don't want to be unconscious anymore. Just saying this makes you conscious. After that initial step, you can accelerate your passage from emotion to emotion by doing the program in the next chapter.

8

A Simple Guide to Emotional Healing

HEALING MADE SIMPLE

1. Give yourself permission to acknowledge and, without resistance, fully experience the emotion.
2. Identify the "trigger" and memories associated with the emotion.
3. Honor a time limit.
4. Ask yourself what *you* can do to change the situation.
5. Have faith that your soul will show you the way to heal and have your needs met.
6. Take action.

By now you should begin knowing and loving yourself more than you have in your entire life. You are unpacking your baggage, and in dealing with it, you are on your way to knowing what has to be healed. I hope this guide to emotional healing will take you on a journey of wellness that will serve you for the rest of your life.

1. Give yourself permission to acknowledge and, without resistance, fully experience the emotion.

As you start to come out of unconsciousness and begin healing, it is crucial to stay "grounded" and give yourself loving permission to be present with your emotion. You must own it to heal to the next level. Being able to feel emotion keeps you ALIVE, and not just existing. People who are attentive to their emotions are much more likely to retain their vitality and excitement about living. There will be many, many times when the pull of apathy, grief, fear, anger, and/or pain will make you want to escape back to bed or a hot bath, or a "bed and breakfast." To stay grounded, you must:

- Take time to acknowledge and identify what you are feeling—"Feeling is Healing!" The moment you feel the emotion, it transforms into its returning attribute (as illustrated on the stages of emotional growth ladder). But you must fully feel the emotion without resisting it.
- Pay attention to and respect the wisdom of your heart and body as well as your head. Let them fully guide you through tears, emotion, silence, screams.

- Fully experience the emotion of each healing level without passing judgment on yourself or your feelings.

2. Identify the "trigger" and memories associated with the emotion.

Ask yourself what triggered this particular emotion. In your mind, review the past few hours and re-experience what is causing you to feel the grief, fear, anger, pain, or combined emotions you are feeling right now. Remember all of the events that have caused you to feel this emotion before. Every emotion has specific memories attached to it. Mentally go back through this memory (or memories). I mean really go back. Purge! Stop resisting! Suppressed emotions will destroy you. Let them out.

Believe me, I know how hard this is. If you think you need a support person to help you with this, then do not hesitate to get one. Go to someone you trust such as a counselor, pastor, friend, or family member and let them be there for you. You must go through the "trigger" and the memories to be free, fall in love with yourself, and become well and whole.

Soul Stretching Exercise

Start a "Feelings Diary" in a little notebook you keep handy (maybe in your purse or in your bathroom).

Take ten to fifteen minutes to do the following:

1. Reflect each day on events
   - focus on how they made you feel
   - ponder the feelings
   - write them in your journal

2. Identify positive and negative feelings (naming feelings = power)
   - glad, loving, joyful, warm, close, etc.
   - sad, frustrated, upset, distant, fearful, disappointed, angry
   - suspicious, rejected, unsafe, paranoid
   - keep these in your journal when you feel them and why

Note: Remember that "fine" and "okay" are not emotions or feelings.

You can learn more about yourself by yourself than you ever thought possible through a guy. You can learn to turn all the aggravation he causes you into enthusiastic ways to learn about yourself. For example, here's one of my first diary entries:

His behavior	What I Usually Do	What I Never Do	What Would Real Love Do?
Stays on computer forever	*Get frustrated, take it personally*	*Realize it has nothing to do with me.*	*1. Go enjoy a movie with a friend, or*
			2. Give him an option: 30 more minutes on the computer in exchange for 30 minutes of snuggling together in front of the TV.

Now that you have become aware of your emotions by feeling and naming them, you must now validate yourself for having them. Be gentle with yourself and look at your emotions without trying to resist them. By experiencing each emotion with love and compassion for yourself, you will be able to move to acquiring Real Love and peace.

3. Honor a time limit.

Fully experiencing an emotion need not mean wallowing in misery and suffering days on end or inflicting your emotions on others. Give yourself a specified amount of time each day to be alone and express your feelings. Everyone is different. Some of you need hours, some minutes; at one point, I gave myself thirty minutes a day for two months. Go totally and completely into the emotion at the level you are working on and stay there. Having a time limit will keep you from obsessing.

If you do this, you will be able to keep yourself together the rest of the time. You can "lose it" in a hot shower, on a long walk, or in your closet. Once your time is up, wash your face and do something nice for yourself before proceeding with "life as usual."

I know some of you are thinking you couldn't possibly give yourself time like this. You can. Human beings—both men and women—can manage by themselves when they have to or want to and they can actually respect each other's need for individual time. Even little children know this. Always make it a win-win situation, and you won't go wrong. If at first you feel uncomfortable about wanting some time for you, then plan something special with your partner or family when your time alone is done.

Everyone will manage, and your partner will notice that you are respecting your needs. This is all part of his education process. Being noticed is a beginning step to getting his attention.

4. Ask yourself what you can do to change the situation.

Let's say the time limit you set for yourself is just about up. You are tired of feeling the way you do, but you can't seem to let go of it. If you really don't feel that you can get past this emotion, then go ahead and say out loud—"I am going to have this emotion forever! So now what do I do?" Bam! You face it head on like that, and you will immediately feel better. You have taken that emotion as far as it can go and you will now begin to shake it loose, so that its healing attribute can help lead you to focusing on what you can do to make a difference.

Do not waste one second trying to figure out what another person should do to change. You will stay sick or get sick if you keep trying to change someone else. Once you shift your thoughts to what your needs are and what you can do for yourself, you instantly switch to finding the positive meaning your emotion was trying to tell you. As soon as you direct your attention to you, you will hear the healing message of your inner voice. Trust yourself.

5. Have faith that your soul will show you the way to heal and have your needs met.

Your soul has graced you with the power to take loving care of yourself, heal, and meet your own needs. Clarify and define your wishes because you can make them come true. Feeling each of your desires in your heart causes creative energy to start flowing towards them. Listen to your inner wisdom as it brings you truth and clarity of what action to take.

6. Take action.

Change your behavior. Do not sabotage yourself by going back to old patterns that were not working for you. Let go of the past. Follow your inspiration. Use your creativity. Don't look back. Only look forward. Take action to change.

As you learn to recognize and work through apathy, grief, fear, anger, pain, and all their associated emotions, you will reach the emotional level of Real Love. It will probably happen when you least expect it, but it will happen. And when you finally reach that beautiful level of love and enthusiasm, you will find that you have reaffirmed a faith in your soul, and yourself, that you never dreamed possible. You will understand what it truly feels like to breathe from your soul instead of only from your chest. You will relish living your life from the emotions of love, enthusiasm, and joy instead of fear, anger, and pain!

I realize I am probably overwhelming you about now. Hang in there. At this point in your journey, simply saying to yourself that you love yourself, you are whole, you are well, or you have found yourself, will not work. It is definitely a start in the right direction. But actually finding wholeness, health, and happiness for yourself and your relationships takes knowing how to do it and then doing it.

It Takes Strength to Feel a Friend's Pain; It Takes Courage to Feel Your Own

Now let's look at each stage of primary emotion to help you understand how to implement emotional healing in your own life. (Refer back to the Wellness Ladder on page 117 when needed.)

Unconsciousness

For fifteen years my life with my husband was like that great country song, "Just Call Me Cleopatra, Baby, Because I'm the Queen of Denial."

Those of you who are having real trouble connecting with what I'm saying are probably either in relationships with extremely emotionally conscious men or may be living at an emotionally unconscious level. I finally snapped out of denial by realizing that when the going gets tough, the tough get growing! I had a lot of growing to do and there was no way my husband was going to grow unless I demanded it of myself first. I had to remind myself of the basic premise from the last chapter: Most men value a woman no more than she values herself. So, first you must operate as a "whole" person and validate yourself. For a while this takes constant effort. Eventually it will become natural. At that point you will never again want to be any other way.

You know that you're operating at an unconscious level if you're constantly using words such as "I don't have any problems," "I couldn't ever say that," "I don't know what you're talking about," or "I don't know, I don't know." When we go through life on an unconscious level, we live our lives day after day doing basically the same things, not feeling, and certainly unaware of and not paying attention to any feelings that we might have.

An unconscious person is in denial of what damage her childhood and past relationships might have caused. She goes through the motions of living, operating at a level much lower than her actual potential. She focuses on routine and not feeling as ways of staying safe. If anyone asks her if something is wrong or how she feels about something, she is truly perplexed. Everything is "just fine" and "whatever you want is all right," so why is anyone asking?

Every unconscious person receives a wake-up call, and, if she does not pay attention, she will receive a whole series of them. These calls may be dramatic such as an illness, the breakup of a relationship, or the death of a family member. They may be other stress-inducing events such as the birth of a baby, a move to a strange town or a job change. They may also come in ordinary packages—the chance remark of a friend, a book such as this one, or a dream. If you pay attention to the call, you will begin fluttering between being unconscious and being apathetic as you progress toward consciousness. This, believe it or not, is progress.

As you know, one of my "wake-up calls" was the "blue robe incident." And as I slowly came to the realization of ever so slight consciousness, I was completely overwhelmed! I would start each morning trying to be conscious of what I was doing with my life and why. Quite frankly, by half past nine in the morning, I would be exhausted and automatically protect my tired mind and body by rising to the level of apathy. Yes! I was progressing.

Even though I could only stay truly conscious and present for about one-and-a-half hours every day, that was long enough to start triggering the emotional healing process. Something powerful happened.

Normally during this time I would get up, get dressed, eat a bowl of cereal, take my birth control pill, and then go to work. The automatic taking of the birth control pill began haunting me during my conscious moments. I had been taking this pill on an unconscious level for over ten years. I had never been emotionally conscious enough to question whether or not this was healthy or, most importantly, if I wanted another child. I also realized I had never even discussed this with my husband. I simply popped the pill every morning.

I made one (this was all I could handle at the time) very conscious decision. I moved my birth control pills from my bathroom shelf to the kitchen counter. Because I was not whole enough to have a loving discussion with my husband about having a second baby, I told him I would not take the pill again until we visited my doctor together and learned the health risks and benefits and made a conscious decision about when and if we wanted to be parents. I asked him to be responsible for birth control until that point.

I think he actually believed that becoming a daddy would be a heck of a lot easier for him than having to go to my gynecologist with me. He told me he did not need to visit my doctor because he already knew it would be best for me not to take the pills any more and, by the way, he would kind of like to have a baby, and, in addition, did I want to have one, too?

I answered, "Sure."

This semi-awakened conversation was our very first attempt at consciousness. Because I changed what I did, he had to wake up a tiny bit, too. Can you begin to see how powerful we women can be as change agents in our relationships?

As a result of this little hour and a half window of consciousness and my first faltering step towards emotional healing, my husband and I were gifted with a beautiful baby boy. Children are one of our clearest messages that love is the level from which we are all intended to live. I didn't know it then, but I know this now. Wherever you bring consciousness, you bring Real Love.

Apathy

After only a short time of being conscious each morning, I was so bone-tired I would switch off—not all the way back to unconsciousness, but to the next level of emotional healing—apathy. At the time, of course, I had absolutely no idea that by sliding into an apathetic state, I was actually doing something my soul had been trying to show me for over thirty years!

When operating at the level of apathy, a woman finds herself using the pronoun "I" accompanied by "not" words about everything—I can't, I don't, I wouldn't, I shouldn't, I couldn't. With these words she communicates her feeling that she is at the mercy of invisible forces and that the external world operates without any help from her. She tells herself things like, "Yes, that relationship ended, but that's not my fault. I'm very unhappy, and I know I did X, Y, Z that probably contributed to things, but it's not my fault."

In the state of apathy, a woman experiences glimpses of consciousness enabling her to crawl towards wholeness even if she does not know it. Feelings begin to penetrate the numbness and denial if only momentarily. The gift that feeling the emotion of apathy gives her is the return of caring. In other words—telling herself that she doesn't care can force her to realize that, in truth, she *does* care. To move on, however, she must realize that staying in apathy is her fault (i.e., her responsibility) and that she is the only person capable of moving herself to the next level.

My job led me to the realization that I was responsible for staying in apathy. Remember my ninety-minute morning consciousness period that threw me into apathy? Well, I had no trouble remaining very apathetic to which cereal I ate for breakfast or what clothes I put on. I was not taking birth control pills any longer, so I had definitely become apathetic about that issue. But my attempts to be apathetic about my job were foiled at every level. My inner conversation went something like this:

Head: "I can't stand teaching night classes. I am a tired, lousy professor after six o'clock in the evening. But it's not my fault I'm teaching night classes."

Heart (which I could barely hear since I had never listened to her before): "Sweetie, it is your responsibility to stand up for yourself and say you'd prefer to teach only during the day."

Head: "Surely I teach at night because I love my job."

Heart: "You are responsible for recognizing how really bored you are at work and how you no longer find it even slightly challenging."

Head: "This is my department director's fault. Anyway, I don't care, and it doesn't really matter. So there!"

I began to get depressed and sad at work. So, one day I was standing with my husband waiting for an elevator when I blurted out, "I would really like to go to law school." I had become conscious enough to be inspired by my mother (the genius of our family), who had raised five kids and then, without blinking an eye, went back to school to get a doctorate. Talk about amazing!

Jim looked at me with a combination of fear and amazement in his eyes and said it was my own fault if I did not go. Certainly not words of loving encouragement, but, of course, I did not care. It was all I needed to hear to make me go to law school and start clawing my way out of apathy towards grief. (Naturally, once I got into law school, there were several days I wished he had just pushed me down the elevator shaft.)

This moving-out-of-apathy elevator conversation forever changed the way my husband saw me, and, more importantly, how I saw myself. In those moments, he saw someone stronger and braver than the Cheryl he knew. I saw someone who had been asleep at the wheel forever and finally woke up.

Grief

Making the decision to leave my stable, boring, well-paying job to go to law school sent me smack into grief. I could not stop myself. My first reaction towards grieving the lost and hurt parts of myself was a feeling of being overwhelmed. As soon as I felt grief, I protected myself by either going unconscious (i.e., numbing out) or becoming apathetic (i.e., Why should I care?).

But my inner voice, the soul I was hearing for the first time, and my body's wisdom, that I was paying attention to for the first time, would not allow me not to care. For two months, I spent an hour each day grieving for the girl who had been fractured and had lost so many pieces of herself that she didn't have enough self-esteem, or care enough about herself, to consider what she really wanted in her life until she was over thirty years old. That girl could never be angry, never be a tomboy, never be upset or proud or difficult, or even just be happy to be a girl. I grieved for all the wholeness she lost and for the assertive, strong, self-confident young woman she could have been. Let's face it. Even if your parents or caregivers were terrific, somehow, some way, somebody did a real number on your self-esteem when you were a kid. All of us have invisible fractures.

But do you see what a miracle this grieving really was? It was giving me back the fractured parts of myself. It was the path to becoming whole. I had to find the young girl who was buried in my unconsciousness for years. Not only did I have to find her, I had to know her, understand her, and learn to love her before I could grieve for her. For the first time in my life, I was cherishing myself by finally acknowledging and validating parts of me that had "gotten misplaced" or "temporarily lost" over the years.

When operating out of grief, a person feels justified in her suffering and is often depressed or bored. She is at high risk for alcohol and drug use and at high risk for getting stuck in her martyrdom.

I learned that consciously resisting the urge to go back to my typical way of dealing with grief (being unconscious or apathetic) allowed an amazing process to unfold. By truly experiencing the incredible sadness and depression of grieving, and being willing to let it go rather than stay stuck in it, I slowly moved from grieving the past to grieving the present. The present? What was happening?

Healing was happening! I was beginning to understand that I had to peacefully put the prior version of myself, the fractured part, to rest in order to be reborn. Although not quite trusting the new self that was emerging, I felt like celebrating this glorious feeling of rebirth! My tears of grief switched to tears of joy! I was not sure about all of this, but it felt so right! I realized I could decide never to be numb or apathetic towards life again. I could choose to put previously suppressed feelings and actions back in my life. By grieving for the lost young woman I could have been, I had learned to love, cherish, and learn from her. She was teaching me what I needed to do to become whole! I would find my self-esteem, inherent worthiness, loves, dislikes, needs, joys, and passions. I would never again say, "I failed," "I can't," or "poor me." I was so determined, so passionate, so excited—and suddenly, so scared!

I had pulled myself out of grief, and now I was afraid. I was experiencing fear. I had not let myself feel it in so long (remember, I was unconscious) that I almost didn't recognize it. But now that I was starting to become whole, fear was a lost feeling that I needed to reclaim and deal with. Now was the time. Besides, my soul was giving me no choice.

Fear

I was taking so many brave steps into emotional consciousness that it was inevitable that I would become afraid. When you start the journey to wholeness, your soul knows when you've become strong enough to go to the next level. You do everything you can at the stage you are at, honor yourself enough to grow, and when you are ready, your soul shoves you onward.

When you are in fear, you expect the worst to happen. I was consumed by the question "What if?" What if law school doesn't work out? What if I can't find time to study? What if my husband doesn't understand the newer, healthier me? What if something is wrong with the baby? What if I become "me"? What if he doesn't love that me? I was becoming paralyzed by fear. Fear was keeping me from truly enjoying law school, from intimately sharing my life with my husband, from marveling at being pregnant! It seems I was always compromising so I wouldn't have to face my fears. I instinctively knew that to truly love myself and others, I needed to quit resisting all my fears, dive headfirst into them, and then move out of fear as soon as possible.

I handled fear the same way I handled apathy and grief. I felt it and faced it head on. I made myself wake up thirty minutes earlier every morning. During these extra minutes, I talked to myself about anything I was afraid of in the coming day. I directly addressed these issues and then outlined the worst that could happen—I might have to repeat a course (but

I will finish law school). My partner might not understand me for a while (but to not understand me, he has to be thinking about me). The baby may have complications (but I'm going to have a baby!). And on and on and on.

I learned two very important things during fear. First, I could never feel happy if I dwelt on "I can't" or "poor me." Never again. Second, if I stayed fearful long enough, I would get what I feared. When I was afraid in law school, my test scores were lower. When I was afraid of what my husband's feelings would be towards me, our relationship was difficult because I withdrew from him. When I worried about the baby, his activity in my womb decreased. Once I felt and faced my fears, I realized I was no longer afraid. I was no longer spending my time trying to keep everyone happy so I wouldn't have to face my fears (a thankless job, by the way).

So you have left unconsciousness and felt at least a little bit alive. You have left apathy and quit saying, "It's not my fault" and have begun to care, and you have pulled yourself out of grief, because you have found the joy in owning your power to heal and have said, "I am not a victim." But now you have reached the level of fear. At this level you tend to disassociate from the pain by retreating and putting up walls to guard against the unknown possibilities of "What if?"

To move out of fear requires pulling down the walls so that the fear can be faced and fully felt head-on. Fear keeps you concentrated on everything that could go wrong. Facing your fears will move you to the next stage, anger, because you finally have the faith and confidence to let your anger out.

Anger

When you examine your fears closely, you realize several things:

1. They haven't happened yet—they are in the future and exist only in your mind.

2. They arise from things you have learned in the past, mainly from messages you received from parents, teachers, boyfriends, friends, Madison Avenue, and Hollywood while you were growing up.

3. Ultimately, the problem is not so much that you were given these messages, but that you believed them!

This is why facing your fears provokes anger—you fell for a line. You were conned into believing you were "less than" in the equation of life. And that can make you pretty darn angry because now you have to undo all those messages, figure out, and rebuild what you truly believe about yourself. You have to change that equation to "equal to" a full, complete, and joyous life. Being really angry at something and feeling that anger helps you understand the problem. True understanding will make it clear to you what has been making you so mad and also how you are doing this to yourself repeatedly. The greatest attribute working through anger gives you is an understanding of what loving action you should take to keep from doing this to yourself over and over again. Most of us feel angry because in some way we have lost power or respect in our relationship.

You will be angry at all the people who fed you those lines in the past and you will become angry at anyone in the present who provokes the same feelings. To heal, it is essential to feel and release the anger. Otherwise, you will project all the hurts and anger from the past onto the people you want to love (and the ones you want to love you) in the present.

As with the other levels, fully experience your anger in a safe way. As you have probably figured out by now, honor yourself with private time to go through this level. I have a dear friend who uses the lovely imagery of watching a candle float down a river as she mentally observes her hurts drifting peacefully away. I wish I had her class! I always need something physical. I tend to want to trash things.

It took months for me to figure out how I could release the anger welling up inside me. First, I needed to get my husband out of my way and get him to take over the parenting duties long enough for me to get out of the house and blow off steam by myself for a while. I can help teach you how to do this lovingly and firmly later, but at that point in my life I didn't have those skills. So quite frankly, what always worked was for me to stand right in front of him so that he could plainly see I was about to snap, and then I would grit my teeth and say, "Unless you want to risk getting exposed to all this estrogen that's flying off me, you'd probably better take over dinner and the kids until I get back. I'll see you in two hours." Jim couldn't get me out of the house fast enough. I would go somewhere and throw over fifty aluminum cans against an old garage wall (they didn't even have to be smashed afterwards at the recycling plant). Then I took a cold shower and screamed; then, a hot shower and cried. Then I wrote down everything I kept bottled up from my past and also explored how I had let my anger unfairly affect my relationship with my husband. I then wrote down everything that I had let my husband do that really pissed me off because I had been too much of an accommodator to tell him. I piled all my confessions in the driveway and torched them with a laser lighter. For days afterward, I drove over the ashes of my past. It felt really good!

After that, however, I discovered something else that works as an anger-release agent for me—amusement park rides, especially roller coasters. I can scream, yell, cry, and act like a complete fool, and guess what? No one even notices. It's wonderful! I feel like a new woman every time I get to ride. But what really makes me feel like a new woman is recognizing my newfound level of confidence in the presence of anger. Anyone else's anger used to make me feel so worthless and ashamed. I actually believed that their anger meant that I was not doing my job. I was not keeping them happy. I had to take charge of my heart and commit myself to only dealing with my anger. If you can get to your anger, you win. You will continue healing and becoming whole.

But now! If someone is angry at me, I am absolutely unwilling to be angry at myself. I know they are not angry with me, they are angry with themselves. In a loving way, I ask them to be responsible for their own anger. It is no longer my job to make them happy. If I had kept wasting my time telling them why they should not be angry and why they are wrong to be angry, then they would commit to proving to me how right their anger was. This is totally self-destructive.

Once I realized this, my anger was going, going, gone. But what's this? I was suddenly hit with an emotion unlike any other. My soul knew I was ready for the first time in my adult life to handle pain—I mean real pain.

Pain

You can keep trying to suppress your pain by shopping, eating, taking pills, whatever. But you must be willing to feel your pain or it will come out as antagonism toward someone else. Your husband, family, and friends do not deserve this.

The good part of arriving at the stage of pain is that you are feeling, and without truly feeling your life, you cannot truly live. Pain is lifesaving! Although you may still lapse into unconsciousness or apathy, you do not remain there long. Fear and anger still arise but no longer drive you. You may eventually taste moments of love, glimmers of what lies ahead. I sometimes felt I was in a hurricane of emotion, spinning around in a pain/anger/fear cycle. Even while experiencing the pain of all these cycles, trust that you *will* gather the strength to spin off towards love. To do so requires the willingness to forgive. Forgiveness is the road out of pain.

While in this stage, I poured my inner being into daily and nightly prayers. I prayed outside under the stars, I prayed as I watched the sun set, I prayed when I couldn't sleep. I prayed when I hurt so much I could not talk. I prayed for the courage and strength to live from love. I could feel myself healing. I could feel the power of getting closer and closer to love and forgiveness and being forgiven.

I view forgiveness as a gift of grace from a higher power. However you explain it, we all carry the ability to forgive within us. But remember that forgiveness does not mean making excuses for someone. Forgiveness must come completely from the love within your heart. It is not something you can "think through." Evidence shows that if you can forgive, then you will enjoy better mental health and physical health. People who continually hold grudges get sick. Refusal to forgive is much more common in angry, fearful, depressed people (the old chicken or the egg problem?). As you would expect, women with the highest self-esteem readily forgive themselves and others.

I do know that the decision to forgive is one of the most freeing and incredible feelings you can experience.

Once you make the decision to forgive, your feelings will take action for you. It will be done. When you forgive someone, you are finally saying you are no longer looking to that person to make you okay. You are making the decision to look to yourself to live your own life and make things right for you. You no longer feel the burden of trying to get the other person to see things your way. Once you can honestly and truly forgive those who have trespassed against you, and once you can honestly and truly forgive yourself, then you can move to Real Love. You will no longer be a slave to fear, anger, or bitterness.

Real Love

Real Love promotes wellness. When you live your life from Real Love, you experience life fully and enthusiastically. Because you were brave enough, courageous enough, and strong enough to go through the levels of emotional healing, you live saying, "I accept it all! I can, I will, I create. I love, I am loved, I am lovable."

Living your life from love means that you are now feeling what it is like to be whole. For me, this resulted in two remarkable changes in the way I related to my husband. First, I began acting and reacting out of love—for me and us. Secondly, I asked myself, How can I use my Real Love to go all the way with this guy and totally disarm him? (As you'll see in the coming chapters, I really have fun with this one.) Real Love enables you to see your mate's positive side, even when he is at his most obnoxious. The things that Jim did that used to hurt and make me furious when I was in Surreal Love made me think he was absolutely adorable when I fell back in love with him through Real Love.

But before you move on, here is how you can make sure to keep on the track of Real Love and never return to a fractured state of emotional unhealthiness.

9

It Takes Strength to Love. It Takes Courage to Be Loved

WHAT WOULD REAL LOVE DO?

To make sure you are living your life as a woman who is whole, the question you should ask yourself in any situation is "What would Real Love for myself do now?" I promise you—if you ask yourself this question as a healing, emotionally-growing, and reaching-for-wholeness woman, you will never go wrong. You are absolutely, without a doubt, becoming more of your own self. As Marjorie Shaevitz beautifully points out in her book, *The Confident Woman*, good things happen when you become more of your own self.

First of all, you feel alive, with an enthusiasm for life and love unlike any you have ever known. Secondly, becoming your real self makes you happier and more naturally loving. Shaevitz states that when you are filled from within, you give from overflow, not from duty or deficit. Third, when you develop Real Love for yourself, you will feel free! You won't look to others for approval or permission because you are now the creator of your own actions. Lastly, as you become more of yourself, you begin to be a causer in life rather than a person being caused. When you are a causer, you are much less likely to be exploited, manipulated, or used. You can stand up for yourself when someone acts disrespectfully toward you, or is demeaning or condescending. Living your life as a self-actualized, self-loving woman is the only way to thrive in a committed relationship.

When my husband and I were having relationship difficulties, I always confused myself (and him) by trying to find answers to the wrong questions. Should I leave, or should I stay? How can I keep from making him mad? How can I avoid hurting his feelings? How can I make him love me again? Yuck! Now that I am whole, I only ask, "What do I feel, do, or say that results in love for who I am, what I stand for, and what I believe in?" I center and calm myself by silently asking this question. This keeps me from acting or reacting straight from apathy, grief, anger, fear, or pain.

Telling you to love yourself and be whole is easy. Explaining how to do it is difficult. It's also very easy to say you now love yourself and you are whole. But actually acting on that is a very different matter. So let me give you the basic scenario that goes on between me and my inner voice during difficult times that I used to let fracture me, and then show you how that same scenario is handled from my present, more whole state. By changing the "same ole, same ole" dynamic of our relationship, my husband had to follow my lead if he wanted to "keep the peace," so to speak.

Difficult time #1,294 before I began the journey to wholeness:

"The Forgotten Promise"

Scenario—For my birthday present my husband promised me a weekend at Lake Toxaway, just the two of us.

Six months later, still no trip. So I ask when I might get my birthday present. I'm really looking forward to it. Of course he can't answer like a secure human being and say something like, "Honey, I have been so busy that I have been negligent to you and us! Forgive me! I'll start planning our trip tomorrow. I can't wait for us to have some time together. Come here and give your senile dude a big hug."

Instead, the insecure guy feels immediately threatened and inadequate that he totally forgot he promised you the trip. Then he makes you feel even worse by saying something stupid like, "Well, I took the whole family to the beach. Doesn't that count?" By saying this he tries to obliterate you in two ways: 1.) He lets you know that time alone with you wasn't his priority as you had hoped, and 2.) He tries to make you feel as if you are such an ungrateful little wench for not letting the family beach trip be your birthday present. (I can guarantee he never mentioned your birthday one time on that whole trip.)

So even though you spent at least seven days showing and telling him how glorious the beach trip was, he now tries to answer your sweet birthday request with, "Well—wasn't that family trip three months ago good enough for you?" In my pre-whole state, I meekly answered "Yes" and I felt bad for bothering him.

"The Forgotten Promise"—after I began my journey to wholeness

Now—same scenario, but this time my response will be that of a healed, whole woman. This time when he answers, "Well—wasn't the family trip three months ago good enough for you?" I pause—before I answer, I must confirm love for myself and ensure I am answering from a loving, whole state of well being. Here I go:

Inner voice (to me):	"I love me (I am not being conceited, self-centered, boastful, etc.; I am acting from a level of love for me)."
Inner voice (to me):	"What do I really feel, after listening to my heart and body? I feel it's time to go for it and neutralize his behavior. I see immediately that he is full of it. He's forgotten my present and is trying to make me feel guilty about it."

Out of love for who I am and the respect I deserve, I must look at him and say:

Outer voice (to him):   "I was so counting on us having time together. All I wanted was my much-anticipated birthday trip so I could be alone with my honey. Please let me know when we are going this month."

Then to complete the disarmament, I run up to him, hug him tightly, and kiss him like he's the cutest thing God ever put on this earth.

He had the trip planned two days later.

YESTERDAY IS HISTORY. TODAY IS A GIFT.

Living your life from love means "Forgetfulness." In other words, forget:

- Trying to get him to see things your way
- Thinking he will change
- Blaming him, fearing him, complaining about him to others
- Holding grudges about the past

The only thing to remember is "What would Real Love for myself do now?"

Living your life from love, anything is possible. Your heart will feel full of joy. You will be amazed at how much higher your threshold for worry, pain, and annoyance will be. You will be shocked at how much lower your risk for depression and health problems will be. Through love, you promote your own self-wellness. And, you can even live happily ever after with your man.

You may be feeling a little overwhelmed again. The thought of getting yourself (much less your mate) on the path to Real Love may seem like an overwhelming task. Instead of focusing on how far the journey may seem, give yourself a huge pat on the back. By reading these five chapters, you have already accomplished the first half of your trip. You are finally beginning to understand why you are standing where you are in your life right now. Things are starting to make sense to you. You are probably still full of self-doubt, but that's only natural and part of the process. By the end of this book, it will be gone.

Now give yourself a little breather. No matter what time of day it is, tell yourself, "I didn't intend to do anything today and so far I'm right on schedule."

The 80/20 Rule

Now is also a good time to point out something else that is very important—the well-known 80/20 rule. None of us can eat right, exercise right, and love right all of the time. I am a firm believer in living your life through moderation. In other words, try to live a healthy lifestyle about 80 percent of the time. Don't sweat the other 20 percent. If you have taken loving care of yourself for 80 percent of the day, then you deserve that Krispy Kreme donut or Hostess cupcake during your 20 percent down time. It's good for your mental health.

The same theory applies to this book. Hopefully, you can apply it in your life and your relationship about 80 percent of the time. I promise you it will be worth the effort. But also give yourself a break. If you feel like you said or did something wrong, or you acted about as non-loving as you've ever acted, forget it. Chalk it up to the 20 percent of the time you and everyone else make mistakes. Just try to keep it to around 20 percent.

You are actually so strong that you are ready to begin the next part of your journey. You have chosen commitment. You know having Real Love in your relationship is where you want to go. You have a goal. All you need to complete this second half of your trip is to learn to think, and then love, using your new brain and your wholeness.

SOUL STRETCH

Okay, prop up your feet, take a deep breath, and relax. It's time to find out if you have passed Basic Training. First, look deep inside and feel your spirit as you take and release each breath. Secondly, write down five words that describe you at this very moment on your journey of life:

1. _____
2. _____

3. _____
4. _____
5. _____

Thirdly, if you are now wearing a grin or a smile (even a little one), you have passed Basic Training for Self-Wellness.

If you aren't smiling, don't be dismayed. You are experiencing the most important chapters of your life. As you know, my search for self-wellness took years. It is my hope that by reading this book your healing will occur at a much faster rate. As you start regaining your emotional wholeness, one day you will suddenly realize that you're not actually working at achieving self-wellness anymore. It's just happening! You did it! You found, connected, and joined your soul into a state of wellness. Thank goodness there's no turning back. Your oneness with yourself, *your empowerment*, is in loving control. That's when you find yourself grinning for no apparent reason. That's when you know you're ready to start taking the lead towards Real Love in your relationship.

What does "taking the lead" towards Real Love really mean? It's actually quite simple. Real Love is being able to make another person feel, even for just a moment, that you love them more than you love yourself. Only a person who has Real Love for herself first is able to give this gift to another. This is why relationships have seemed so damn hard. They have notoriously been based on Surreal Love. Sure, you were always taking care of his needs, being nice when you didn't feel like it, and accommodating everyone but yourself. That was loving another more than yourself, wasn't it? Your partner should have felt your love from all you did for him, right?

The answer is—no way! Previously, you were being nice out of Surreal Love. As you've learned, that is your weakest place. Others feel your Real Love only when you're coming from the strength of your own Real Love. The behavior changes that you want in your partner are only possible because, with your Real Love for yourself strongly in place, you can now use the skills, humor, and information in the next four chapters to let him know you accept and love *him*. You just don't accept and love some of his behaviors. This is a huge difference in your relationship. Only when a man knows (by feeling your Real Love) that he is acceptable and lovable will he be able to change his behavior.

These next chapters will show you how to use your Real Love to help him feel accepted and loved while you take the lead in the relationship. While Surreal Love tends to be a little selfish, tries to be perfect, and concerns itself with meeting "old brain" ego needs and validating self-worth, Real Love is gloriously and simply human. Real Love has the strength to see and forgive faults. To have Real Love, you must know your boundaries. Only with this knowledge can you let your boundaries of self sometimes safely and beautifully blur with your partner as you become one. Even if just for a few seconds you are able to feel his pain and pleasure as if they were your own, you will know Real Love. You will finally feel a higher form of love, a love that helps redeem your relationship from brokenness.

Enjoy the next section. Now that you have Real Love for yourself, you are a "Wild Woman!" You love yourself enough now that if what you do with your man works, then great! If it doesn't, it will still wake him up a little. And if you make a total fool of yourself, then celebrate the fun you had doing it! Now let's go get him!

Wa–Wai–Wait–*Wait a minute*! I can't let you go charging off to the next section yet. I've got to be fair to you. I have to keep being open and honest with you. I must share with you what was going on with me right at this juncture of my life. I need to tell you how my becoming more whole made me feel towards Jim.

My old brain is yelling, "Don't tell them, don't go there, too fearful, not safe—"

My new brain is very calmly saying to my old brain, "It's okay. Our girl is healing up nicely. Let her tell her readers the truth. The truth shall set her free and help others."

My old brain shouts back, "The truth will piss her husband off and you know it! This is not safe. Not safe!"

But since I have Real Love for myself now, my new brain is in control so that I have the confidence and faith I need to proceed. Here goes.

After I did everything I've described, I started to feel like a new person. Being close to wholeness made me feel closer to living, laughing, loving, knowing, being! Healing felt so damn wonderful! Living my life through love instead of fear felt absolutely glorious. I thrilled at having Real Love for myself and couldn't wait to share Real Love with my partner.

Enter Jim.

Time for a serious reality check. After I was healed, I can remember sitting across from him at the dinner table, watching his mouth move, and all I kept thinking was, What in the world do I do now? I have two kids who I love more than life itself, and one man who I can barely tolerate anymore. I mean, on a scale of one to ten, my tolerance level for Jim was about .02. Oh man! I had some serious work to do to fall in Real Love with this guy I had married.

I had to understand why I was feeling this way towards him. He was basically the same guy now as he was when I married him. Bingo! Herein lies the key to the healing ability of understanding the I.D.I.O.T. theory.

First of all, internal cues and timing weren't the problem. They had matured from being interrelated to getting married to being an integral part of the biological and social expectations of being a family. As I continued to feed my little baby and watch Jim and my older son eat their dinner, I felt good. No alarms went off. I was married, employed, and I loved being a mother. I was blessed with a beautiful family.

Back to Jim.

He was definitely still handsome. In fact, to me, he looked pretty darned near perfect. But he wasn't so damn cute any more. Now I was getting somewhere. A few alarm bells were starting to sound. Why didn't he seem "cute" anymore? Intuitively, I knew it had nothing to do with his physical appearance. It was something to do with—with—what?

"Cheryl," my new brain rationally states, "you have worked very, very hard to get to where you are now. You feel a healing and a wholeness that you never thought possible. In fact, you continue to be amazed at how well you can hear my loving voice on a daily basis. Now think hard, Cheryl. Why do you feel Jim doesn't seem as 'cute' to you anymore?"

I slowly but surely came to the realization that my tolerance level for my husband and his cuteness meter were both almost zero because he was a distant, condescending know-it-all. He dressed better than I did. He loved being a doctor and being so smart all the time. He was controlling. He was—"For crying out loud!" shouts my old brain. "Those are the pieces you needed to be whole! He had 'em, you wanted 'em, so I got 'em for ya! You wanted a doctor who could ensure your survival socially and financially. Call it surreal, call it loving under false pretenses, call it a felony for all I care. You thought I was doing a great job when you were dating him and just 'haaad to have him or you would absolutely die,' but I can already feel you gathering your strength to shut me out. Hey, wait a minute—I'm not finished yet. Let's just find another guy who has some attributes you're still working on. We'll feel great again! You'll see. Come on."

With my new brain, I calmed down my old brain fear, anger, and disillusionment that had been building against my partner as I was becoming well within myself. As I watched Jim lean back from the table, I realized how devastatingly crucial it was that I pay attention to what I was hearing and feeling. I continued to silence my old brain with the new brain knowledge that I am secure and safe within myself now. I assured my old brain that "I know what I know." I know that in living my life through Real Love, I will always be able to provide for and protect myself and my family. My old brain finally sends an "all clear" signal to my new brain. Now I can think clearly and figure out what's going on.

Now that I was more emotionally whole, all the traits that I comfortably identified as familiar about Jim when I was dating him (such as being distant, brilliant, and self-centered) were now the very same ones that made me totally irritated with him. My old-brain fears of being criticized, rejected, or considered unlovable weren't fears anymore. I had Real Love for me. I knew I had the gift of being able to love like I had never been hurt. No one could ever make me feel unlovable again. In fact, I felt so loving towards my newly empowered self that I realized that I deserved a better relationship, a more emotionally present partner, a more loving and thoughtful partner. Jim wasn't any of these at this point and this made him not only clueless, but also totally "uncute." In fact, our relationship with each other had seemed to hit rock bottom. The more whole I became, the more my eyes were open to what was real about us.

Now it's time for an "Aha!" moment. I'll tell you what was and is real. It is real to feel this way about your partner after you become more whole. It's actually a sign of your wellness that you can have such an epiphany about the man you married. When he looks that lousy to you, you've got nowhere to go but up. So as Jim burped and said his usual, "Now can we have dessert?" I took myself up to a level of Real Love and looked at him only as I could now that I was healing myself.

For the first time since I'd known Jim, I saw him as he really was at the dinner table that night. Yeah, he was obnoxious and a jerk sometimes. But he sure did love me, and I did love him. He'd stuck by me even though I had been acting really strange the last few years. His commitment to our marriage had never wavered (it was rigid as hell, but it was never questioned). He was a good man and a good father and I was pretty sure he was trainable. Okay. It's a start.

I knew I was strong enough to have my relationship needs met. I knew that since I was able to fall in Real Love with me, I could basically start over, using the messages of my new brain, to fall in Real Love with my husband. As I watched him show the kids how he could slurp Jell-O between his front teeth, I realized that it wasn't going to be easy, but he did look kinda cute making the boys laugh like that. Wow! I said the word "cute." I must be ready to show Jim what Real Love is all about.

Now—let's go get him!

{SECTION IV}

How to Recognize and Treat R.A.D.S. (Relationship Attention Deficit Syndrome)

10

Connecting with the Clueless Male

WIFE DISCOVERS HOW TO GET HER HUSBAND'S ATTENTION EVEN WHEN HE'S NOT LISTENING

Yes, I did it. I didn't mean to, but I was desperate. I could see all the signs and symptoms of developing R.A.D.S. (Relationship Attention Deficit Disorder), and I knew I would have to use some relationship TNT to ever stand a chance at getting his attention during the commercial. So, I took my best shot. I used the "F" word and the "L" word in the same sentence. I can't believe I expected him to respond. We are supposed to build this relationship together, aren't we? Shouldn't we each give at least 50 percent effort to try and make this work?

Why is he still looking at me like I'm from another planet? All I did was ever so gently mention my "feelings" and "love" in trying to explain to him for the thousandth time about a very important problem in our relationship. Surely he knows that I love him so much that it really hurts my feelings when he comes home and goes straight to the computer or television without so much as a little hug for me. I mean, I've been telling him this for twelve years. Can't he understand this problem by now?

I can tell he's trying his best not to let his eyes glaze over. But he knows if he blinks, he'll lose any hope of concentrating on trying to figure out what foreign language this "wife person" is speaking. He knows she's talked this way before and he didn't have a clue what she wanted then either.

Someone help me. What do I do now? He's nodding his head in agreement like he always does when he wants me to think that he's heard me and things will be different. I know better! The nod just means the commercial break is over and the football game is back on. I won't take this anymore!

BEWARE OF R.A.D.S.

My man had Relationship Attention Deficit Syndrome (commonly known as "stonewalling"). You know your man has R.A.D.S. when he's pushing all your buttons more than he's pushing the ones on his remote control. To have a relationship based on Real Love, I needed a partner with whom I could openly and safely share my feelings. I couldn't do this if I couldn't get his attention.

To successfully treat R.A.D.S., I had to 1) devise ways of getting my husband's attention and 2) present a clear and precise plan of action (a solution) to him for his participation. Even if a man is totally clueless, once he learns how and experiences the rewards, he will gladly do it on his own—at least most of the time.

My husband appears to be listening when he is paying absolutely no attention. He has a keenly developed and selective sense of language comprehension. He hears but understands only when and what he wants. He can understand quantum physics or intricate football plays presented by a sportscaster mumbling through a wool muffler, but when I begin to talk, although he may nod and make eye contact, he has no clue. This is particularly true if a feeling response is required. Jim is an expert at retreating behind some sort of protective shield and tuning out. The first survival skill I had to learn—and the one underlying all the others—was how to communicate effectively with my mate.

Dr. Deborah Tannen states that women communicate to connect and accomplish understanding and intimacy. Men see communication as a way of establishing their rank in the hierarchy to maintain power.

Therefore, to get his attention and communicate effectively, I suggest trying to eliminate the hierarchy and the power struggle. By combining your imagination and love with your sense of humor and craziness, you can get his attention, yet he won't feel he's been caught "one down."

In his book *Seven Principles for Making Marriage Work*, Dr. John Gottman emphasizes that it is usually the wife that brings up marital issues for discussion. She also is usually the one who presents an analysis of the problem and suggests solutions. He maintains that when a man is able to accept his spouse's ideas, the relationship has a much better chance to be successful.

Your first step will be to prompt him to crack his protective shield a bit so you can get his attention. This first crack is the hardest and will take determination on your part. Once you create the opening and begin to get his attention so you can implement the other survival skills, he may eventually remove the shield. Then you can get closer to the tender person inside all that isolating armor.

THE SIXTH SENSE?—NOT!

Don't even think of trying to explain to him why and how you feel the way you do. Don't waste your breath, time, and energy trying to help him understand why you are asking him to do a certain thing. The hours I've wasted desperately attempting to get his attention by trying to help him understand would surely add up to years. Don't play Freud. He does not want to be psychoanalyzed. He would only see that as being criticized and that makes him feel inadequate. Don't even go there! Don't forget he's a man! He is incapable of grasping these concepts. These are concepts promoting warmth and bonding between two people. He is not ready for this yet! Hang on. He will be able to bond to some degree by the end of the book. But right now is too early.

Men do not think like we do. Gottman contends that much of this difference begins in childhood where girls are encouraged to gain skill and experience in navigating emotional issues, whereas boys are often socially punished for expressing emotion, particularly as their peer groups socialize. We've got to give them a break on this crucial first step. Since you want his attention, you must speak in his language. In other words, our communication must relate to one or more of his five senses. It must be a communication he can see, hear, touch, smell, or taste. Don't ever expect to get his attention through things such as intuition, internalizing, telepathy, or any other sort of mental connection. He does not have this capacity.

He has an invisible "mute" button on his shield that he can punch while you're talking. If that doesn't work, he can "blip" you right off his visual screen. If you want his attention, you must offer channels different than any he has seen and stimulate one of his five senses. Dr. Gottman's research validates the fact that if you can learn ways to calm yourself, speak and listen nondefensively, and validate your partner and your marriage, you stand a good chance of working through marital trouble spots without causing your man to emotionally withdraw. Here's how I "communicate" with Jim.

Let's start with a play-by-play:

Proceed slowly and calmly.
Otherwise, he will feel attacked and close his shield more tightly. **Example:** Whether he's watching TV or on the computer, never "wake him up" too fast. When he gets scared, he withdraws into

his shell. To make sure he still keeps his head poked out, I always gently begin by touching him very lightly on his arm, shoulder, or hand—nothing too personal, just enough to start to get his attention.

Gently place a small amount of appealing food or something warm to drink in front of him.

This lowers his defenses, stimulates his sense of taste and sight, and gives him something to focus on if he is uncomfortable. At the same time, your gestures cause him to wonder what will happen next.

Example: I like to use hot chocolate and doughnuts in the winter. During the summer, I use golden margaritas and nacho chips. I must say, he likes the summertime "attention-getters" better than the winter ones. This way, if he gets a little nervous, he can chomp loudly on the nacho chips. He finds that to be much more calming than twirling his doughnut.

Do not try to read anything into his silence.

It's just silence. Remain calm and stay nondefensive.

Example: Some of the most ridiculous blabbing I have ever done has been when I have tried to "fill in" periods of uncomfortable silence between Jim and me. I never let silence make me feel uneasy anymore. I actually kind of enjoy just waiting in silence for a few minutes until I'm ready to proceed.

Sit directly across from him; never talk to him from a distance.

Make sure there are no distractions other than the food. Rely on his sight and sound connection. Look directly into his eyes, speak concisely, and ask him to repeat back what he heard. Use the "I" messages.

Example: Instead of saying, "You are not paying attention to me," I try to say, "Maybe I have not communicated clearly what I want you to know." I keep the conversation about me and what I want to communicate, not about him and his shortcomings. A man's ego must be handled with care. He pays attention much better if he doesn't feel he's being criticized.

Never physically or verbally point your finger at him.

This may make him withdraw, just when you are starting to get his attention.

Example: My communication is about my needs. So as I tell him what I need, I gently touch my heart with my fingertips when I feel better doing something with my hands. Later (months or years), I was able to hold his hands as I talked, but not at first. He was not ready.

Finish off with "I would like to hear what you think I just said."

Example: I had to have my husband repeat what he heard back to me for a year before he was ready to listen as an equal partner instead of a man defending his turf.

Here is an example of what I did when I decided my husband and I needed to spend more time together. First, I decided exactly what I wanted and then I chose my moment carefully. He was sitting at the kitchen table sorting the mail. I gently touched his shoulder and told him I would like to talk for a few minutes. I set down a steaming mug of buttered rum for each of us and sat directly across from him. I looked straight into his gorgeous blue eyes and I told him I wanted him to ask his lovely wife out for a date once a week. After a pregnant pause, I asked him to repeat back to me what he had heard. He said, "You want me to ask you out once in awhile." I said, "That's really close, but I must not have stressed the lovely wife part and the once a week part. Would you mind trying again?" This time he got it right. "You, my lovely wife, want me to ask you out, like on a date or something, once a week."

Keep the message on track.
Example: Jim is an expert at trying to divert me with nit-picky details and/or trying to put me on the defensive. Do not let this happen. You must stay in the driver's seat and remain in control. As soon as he tries the "Well—aren't you happy that I took the time to take you to Wal-Mart last week?" Response: Don't even answer that question. Get straight back to your message and stay there.

Sometimes Jim tries to keep confusing the issue, skirting the topic of discussion, and putting me on the defensive. He can be amazingly dense sometimes. Understanding core problems is hard for him. He will go off on a tangent. My husband has yet to understand the moral of *The Bridges of Madison County*. The beauty of once in a lifetime love and passion sailed right past him. He focused totally on the type of camera Clint Eastwood was using back then. (You can tell I had to insist that he go to the movie; the book was out of the question.) Always stick to the bottom line. Never deviate from the core message you want him to understand.

Write down what you want him to pay attention to.

Example: It is crucial that I write down anything that requires his thorough attention. "Remember to pick up Junior at school at three," or "My feelings were really hurt when you gave me a 'Dust Buster' for our twentieth anniversary." Whatever you say to him, make it short and to the point. To be sure he reads every word of my note, I sign off with something like, "Tonight I want to be on top," or "I can't stop thinking about doing it on the kitchen table." Believe me, even a clueless man will reread the note. Have fun letting your own sexy side come out of the closet. This will help validate him and the marriage.

Do a "make him feel good" follow-up reminder.

Write the message down on a Post-it note and put it on his wallet. Then put a note on the door, in his lunch, on the steering wheel, wherever, to remind him to pay attention to the note on his wallet. The trick to these notes is that they must catch his attention. Scientific research shows that if what is being communicated interests the listener, or is meaningful to his life, his capacity to hear it vastly improves. In other words, if what you say or write is a boost to his ego or something he really wants, he will gladly pay attention. Two events which fulfill these criteria for men and make them raise their shields a fraction are sex—not to be confused with "making love"—and sports. Think: Dallas Cowboys

Cheerleaders. You must, therefore, attach to the note either a ticket to some sporting event, or embellish your note with compliments about his sexiness.

Example: I usually begin a note to my husband with, "Hi, Handsome Man," or "Dear Good-Looking Hunk." Remember, with men, such sentiments as, "Dear Love of My Life," or "Dear Soul Mate," don't work nearly as well as an appeal to his physical side. In the first week after my dating request, I decided on the following follow-up. A few days after our "heart-to-shield" talk, I waited until he set out the clothes he was going to wear to work the next morning. After he climbed into bed, I stuck a note right on the zipper of his pants reminding him that Thursday or Friday would be my most favorite night to have a hot date with him. I simply signed the note, "From the one who's stuck on you!" The next morning, he asked me out before he left for work.

Practice the above skills until they are second nature.

IF HE WON'T RISE UP TO YOUR LEVEL, GO DOWN TO HIS

If your first attempts at getting his attention do not have the impact you hoped, you may need to resort to communicating with him on his own level. Be inventive and have a great time. My man likes guns, ammo, any of that testosterone-loaded stuff. I learned to communicate with him by watching the movie

Striptease. Now, I know what you are thinking. Most men come to attention when Demi Moore strips. If I tried it, however, my man would tell me to quit blocking the television. I am referring to the scene where the bouncer at the topless club needs to get his shyster lawyer to pay attention. I did the same scene with my husband and it worked. I bought a black T-shirt and camouflage pants at the Army Surplus Store and added black boots and black shades. I retrieved the cordless power drill from the garage and walked into the den armed with a fully operating power drill held like a well-aimed .45. Believe me, I got his attention. He remembered every word I said!

Many women live with men who are "televisionaholics." There's something about being in a horizontal position with a remote control that makes a man feel invincible. Once again, relate to Captain Couch at a level he can understand. When you really want his attention, make your own "infomercial." Use a video camera (rent or borrow one if need be) and film yourself telling him what you want him to hear *loud* and *clear*. Resort to any and all props you can think of which will keep his attention while you are speaking. In other words, wear a football helmet, wear nothing, brandish a baseball bat, hold a six-pack of beer, or do all of the above.

My hubby used to escape to TV land during special family gatherings, a habit I found very irritating. Several years ago, right before the holidays, I made a ten-minute video of myself talking to a twenty-pound turkey thawing on the kitchen counter. I tucked a television remote control under the turkey's wing so that even you-know-who would get the symbolism. I then made a very passionate emotional plea to my "cold turkey" about how I seriously needed his help, support, and emotional presence during the holidays, explaining in concise words what I meant by this. He agreed to keep the television unplugged during any holiday or family gathering until 11:00 p.m. I agreed to an exception for the January Super Bowl.

Computers also provide men with an escape from relating. When television bores him, my husband spends hours on the computer. For the nights I would like his company, I have made a series of screen savers. I created rotating 3-D color messages saying, "Don't even think about it!" and "Prevent cyber war; be with your wife!"

You deserve having your needs met, so do whatever it takes. Use your imagination, your sense of humor, your craziness! If you are going to stay in a relationship with the guy, then you have a right to demand his attention! You may be tempted to say, "But I shouldn't have to shoulder all the responsibility for this relationship. He should know I need some attention; he should want to be with me." Yes, he should. But remember—he is just a man. He loves you in his way, but he is clueless about what it takes to make a relationship work. Yelling, ranting, raving, and explaining do not work with most men.

PEACEMAKING WE CAN LEARN FROM DOGS

If you have ever taken a dog to training school, you know that first you train yourself. Then you can get the dog to behave as you wish with gentle reminders and plenty of rewards. You learn to be persistent and consistent, to communicate clearly, and to keep your mind on what you want: a loyal pet who will follow commands. Now, I am not saying men are like dogs or that they should come panting when you whistle. I am saying that many lessons about living with men can be learned from observing ever-faithful canine companions. One of the most obvious lessons is that punishments, whether they be verbal reprimands, distancing, or even withholding dinner, absolutely never work. Male creatures love rewards! All obedience schools are based on the reward system, so it's probably worth applying some of their basic principles:

- Remember that what you want is a responsive, attentive companion.
- Be persistent and consistent in teaching him what you expect.
- Communicate your needs clearly.
- Model gentle, loving behavior.
- Lavish him with rewards (which will reward you too!)

My husband and I both work. Nighttimes with my husband are a joke. Here's how we typically "go to bed." Jim's watching TV and I pop my head in the den and say, "I'm tired, and it's getting late. I think I'll go to bed." I go to the kitchen to make sandwiches for the next day's lunches. I rinse out the popcorn bowls and take something out of the freezer for supper the following evening. I check the cereal box and milk levels, fill the sugar container, put spoons and bowls on the table, and hunt down the Ziploc sandwich bags. I then put some wet clothes in the dryer, put a load of clothes into the wash, and secure a loose button. I pick up the game pieces left on the table and put the telephone book back into the drawer. I water the plants, empty a wastebasket, and hang up a towel to dry. I yawn and stretch and head for the bedroom. I stop by the desk and write a note to the teacher, count out some cash for the field trip, and pull a textbook out from hiding under the chair. I write a birthday card for a friend, address and stamp the envelope, and write a quick note for the grocery store. I put both near my purse or otherwise I will have no memory of them. I then wash my face, put on moisturizer, brush and floss my teeth, and trim my nails. Hubby calls, "I thought you were going to bed." "I'm on my way," I say. I put some water into the fish tank and make sure the doors are locked. I look in on each of my sons and turn out a bedside lamp, hang up a shirt, throw some dirty socks in the hamper, and have a brief conversation with the one still up doing homework. In my own room, I set the alarm, lay out clothing for the next day, and straighten up the shoe rack. I add three things to my list of things to do for tomorrow. About that time, Jim turns off the TV and announces to no one in particular, "I'm going to bed." And he does.

But mornings with my husband—that's where I draw the line! Whenever he has a day off, I get up early to get the children ready for school. Whenever I have a day off, I still get up early with the children. This discrepancy was important enough to me that I needed to get his attention. After ten years of getting children ready for school every day, I finally asked him if he would please get up early the next morning and enjoy helping our children before he went to work. I told him how tired I was and how much I would love to sleep in. He looked at me as if I were an unfit mother. He said he could not understand why I was even asking him to do this. I swear, one of these days I'm going to produce my own version of *Survivor*. I will pick twelve men who will be dropped in an unidentified suburb. They will be given a van, six kids (each of whom plays two sports and takes either a musical instrument or dance class), and no access to fast food. They must keep the house clean, correct all homework (receiving at least a "C+" on all papers), complete one science project, cook (okay, they can bring one cookbook), and do laundry. They'll also have access to television only when the kids are asleep and all chores are done. Oh, and none of the TVs will have remotes. Plus they have to shave their legs and wear makeup, which they must apply themselves either while driving or while making six lunches. The competitions will consist of such things as attending a PTA meeting and accurately reporting the results; cleaning up after a sick child at 3:00 a.m.; making an Eskimo igloo with six toothpicks, marshmallows, and one marker; and getting a four-year-old to eat a serving of carrots. The kids vote them off. The winner gets to go back to his job. Anyway, I digress.

It was time to get his attention. I made it clear that my request was fair, reasonable, and deserved a positive response. I lovingly told him I would sleep late, and if he did not want to get up early, the children could be late for school. The next morning, the alarm rang and I stayed in bed. My self-worth was more important than the boys' timeliness.

Moral #1: A man has to learn you mean what you say and that you will not back down.

Finally, after ten minutes of clearing his throat, my husband rose and took care of things.

Moral #2: A man loves food rewards!

When he came home from work that evening, I fixed his favorite supper and dessert. Just to give you an idea of what kind of rewards men like, it helps to know that their food preferences are very different from ours. For example: women are 76 percent more likely to crave chocolate; men are 78 percent more likely to crave meat.

Men are:

76 percent more likely to crave eggs

69 percent more likely to crave hot dogs

10 percent more likely to crave pizza

10 percent more likely to crave seafood

Most likely to prefer:

#1. red meat

#2. pizza

#3. potatoes

Women are:

71 percent more likely to crave crackers

62 percent more likely to crave ice cream

62 percent more likely to crave candy

65 percent more likely to crave fruit

Most likely to prefer:

#1. chocolate

#2. bread

#3. ice cream

Moral #3: Always make him straighten out his own messes. Do not take over and do it for him, or he will never learn.

Another time I had to get hubby's attention involved remembering the few days he was supposed to pick up our children. What I learned from this is that when you call your partner and children to dinner and only he appears, it means that he will swear on Elvis's grave you never told him to pick the children up at day care. Do not bail him out. Have him call the director of the day care center and find out into which foster home your children were placed.

Whenever you try to tell a man what to do, or when he finally figures out he is not getting his way, he may pout. This is one of the few times a man gets "in touch with his inner child." He becomes very quiet, withdrawn, and nothing pleases him. He does not want to play anymore, and he makes certain you know it. That kind of behavior may have been tolerated earlier, but you do not have to put up with it in your relationship now.

I was determined to teach my man that pouting is inappropriate behavior for grown-ups. My first attempt was at our seven-year-old son's soccer game. The day was beautiful. I felt blessed to be watching our little boy play soccer with my husband on one side of me and our one-year-old son on the other. Towards the end of the game, our son, the goalie, was entertaining himself by trying to catch a caterpillar crawling up the soccer goalpost. The ball rolled past him—twice.

As a result, his team lost and the coach was sent off the field for using foul language. But after all, the game is supposed to be fun for the kids, whose main concern is the after-game snack. My husband, however, was solely focused on our son's failure to be a "star athlete." By the time the game was over, he was in full "I'm not happy with this situation" pout. He did not want to talk, or even walk, with any of us.

It was time to get his attention and put a stop to his nonsense. I wanted to have fun and I wanted my kids to have fun. I turned to my pouting husband, looked him straight in the eyes, and told him I was taking the boys out for lunch to celebrate the great soccer game and the acquisition of our new pet caterpillar. I explained I needed him to quit pouting and spoiling our good time. I gave him two, and only two, choices. He could straighten up and enjoy lunch with his family, or he could go home and take a time-out.

Moral #4: Never give a man more than two options. (Some can handle only one.)

He chose lunch. Our boys were merciless with their dad. Any time he got quiet and pouted, they would point at him, laugh hysterically, and do everything from imitating him, to taking bets on how long a time-out I would give him, to throwing sugar-packet bullets at him. Seeing two children act more mature than their father is rather scary and confirmed my suspicion that I was raising three, not two, children.

Sometimes men pout because they need a little space. Whenever you can see even the tiniest bit of justification for this, give it to them. Other times men pout because they need a big hug, a soft cuddle, and a little reassurance. Although rarely exhibited, men do have the ability to be the sweetest, kindest, most wonderful people in the world. Pay close attention to how you feel about why and when he's pouting. If his moodiness has not demeaned or dismissed your needs, then strongly consider snuggling up to him. Do not let the moment slip away! Hold him, hug him, love him. Maybe he will respond with a big smile.

What if you have tried all the above—you have been complimentary, gentle, kind, firm, clear, humorous, entertaining, you've stood your ground and even taught him about rewards—and he still is not acknowledging you by giving you his attention. Believe it or not, you have his attention. He has definitely never seen you act this way before! He is playing hardball by making sure you do not know it. He is not going to crack open his shield even a tiny bit unless he has to. The time has come when he has to. Your self demands (soon to command) it, and his humanhood depends upon it.

Moral #5: Sometimes you have to make consequences known.
First, you may want to try a lighthearted approach to showing him the consequences of his not paying attention. One time when I could not get my husband's attention regarding something very important to me, I knew it was time to make consequences known. My younger son loves the *Magic School Bus* series of children's books, and we have plenty of them around the house. I made a book for Jim of brightly colored construction paper and wrote on the cover, "The Magic School Bus inside Daddy's New Doghouse." My handwritten text, about visiting the poor, lonely Daddy Dog, clearly outlined for him the consequences of his being inattentive to the situation at hand. The book worked. He laughed, but gave me and the problem his immediate attention.

Any time that protective shield is cracked open, even a little, the benefits are wonderful for both of us. I feel so proud of my accomplishment, and he actually gets a glimpse of what it is like to be in Real Love in a relationship.

When you feel this Real Love starting to happen, and you will, enjoy and apply to your partner the other lessons we can learn from the unconditional love of dogs:

1. Never pass up the opportunity to go for a joy ride. Relish the feeling of fresh air and the wind in your face. (Try not to drool.)
2. When your loved ones come home, run to greet them.
3. When it's in your best interest, be sure to tell your sweetie how much you loved following his suggestion.
4. Let him know if he's invaded your territory.
5. Take naps and stretch.
6. Run, romp, and play with him at least once a week.
7. Eat with gusto and enthusiasm.
8. Be loyal.
9. Never pretend to be something you're not.
10. If what you want lies buried, dig until you find it.
11. When he's having a bad day, be silent, sit close, and snuggle with him gently.
12. Thrive on his newfound attention.
13. Avoid barking when a simple growl will do.
14. When you're happy with him, dance around and wag your entire body.
15. Delight in long walks with him.

16. No matter how often he's clueless, don't buy into the guilt thing and withdraw. Run right back, get his attention, and make friends.

After a while a man's continued lack of attention to a matter threatening your relationship is anything but funny. You must learn to apply the steps in this book for yourself first. By doing so, your relationship will shift in unforeseen ways.

This journey is not about changing your man, but about changing your life. He will respond to this process in his own way. My partner began taking many bold, brave baby steps of his own and eventually agreed to counseling.

Some men may continue their deeply instilled habits of inattention longer than others. Be absolutely certain you are prepared to stay patient and to follow through. Remember Moral #1: A man has to learn you mean what you say and that you will not back down.

Your dignity, self-worth, and self-validation depend on it. Backing down from a consequence with a man will only insure that he will never take you seriously. Stick to your guns. Your strength will be your growth. You must say what you mean and do what you say.

Making him pay attention will usually cause most men to create a tiny opening in that blasted armor. Seize the opportunity and you will be ready for the next step of convincing him to keep his head permanently out of his shell. Be ready! Be sure of yourself and your wholeness. He will start connecting with you, although things may get a little rocky before they begin smoothing out.

As long as he was distant and you could be "put off," he felt safe and in control. This kept your relationship in Surreal Love. But now that you have made a little crack in his armor, he is beginning to pay attention and get closer to having a relationship based on Real Love. Beware that he may occasionally revert to being one scared guy. And a fearful man is not a pretty sight. He truly seems to go alien on you. You may be right in the middle of a discussion, and suddenly he seems unrecognizable to you. The words coming out of his mouth sound foreign, unlike any you have ever heard from him. Or his inappropriate silence is accompanied by a look that is so strange you feel like you're watching real life "X-Files."

When he pulls this alien act on you, it is crucial that you show him Real Love by learning how to neutralize his behavior by teaching him to "cut the crap."

11

Teaching Him to Cut the Crap

WOMAN WALKS OUT ON HUSBAND BEFORE FINISHING EXPENSIVE DINNER

Uh oh—my empowerment was showing. I was smiling more. I was being assertive. I was acting differently than I used to. All this was starting to make him feel…feel…feel what?! He doesn't know what. He just knows change is in the air and he is very skeptical and afraid. Now was the time to be sure I understood what was causing him to resort to alien behavior and how to neutralize it.

CAUSATION OF OBNOXIOUS BEHAVIOR IN MEN

I was taking the first steps towards *change*, and change is a man's worst nightmare. Deep inside he knows that a change in you equals a change in the relationship, and he begins to fear he might have to change too. He will resist. This is why I had to be the change agent for both myself and the relationship. While you attempt to march forward, you may feel he is trying to drag you backwards. Stay strong; keep working! You are getting his attention and in most cases, he will not want to risk losing you. Studies have shown over and over that men don't like living alone. They have much more difficulty not being married than women do. But more importantly, you must never risk losing yourself again!

Because feelings fluctuate, they suggest vulnerability and are scary to men. Vulnerability evokes male warrior instincts and causes them to put their guards up. Men only want to deal with what they can control, manage, and take action with or against (even if this omits most of life). A feeling cannot be grabbed; it appears seemingly from nowhere and upsets the balance of the day. A feeling requires self-examination (self-insight is another trait not within the realm of the five senses) and often sounds an alert that change is on the way.

THE TRUE DEFINITION OF "I'M FINE"

When your partner comes home from work, obviously tired and upset, and you respond by asking with concern how his day went, he probably cuts off any hopes of intimate conversation by saying, "Fine," and rushing off to make a drink and/or watch the news. For a man, "fine" usually means he is feeling:

Fed up

Insecure

Neurotic

Egocentric

"Fine" shuts you out without a clue. Is he sick of work? Is he angry that he pays the bills and there is no money left for him? Is he dealing with job insecurity? Who knows? Feelings have crept into his being, causing terrible confusion. His answer is to become Captain Couch (or Grouch) in order to escape. He knows you will want to talk about it and talking about it will force him to face the feelings, his own vulnerability, and the possibility his world may be changing.

My husband can't even be vulnerable when he's sick. He usually sits in his chair in the den in front of the television. Used tissues are strewn all around him in tribute to the Royal Highness of Mucous. His voice is reminiscent of one of the Munchkins in *The Wizard of Oz* and even Rudolph would pale in comparison to this nose. I wait on him hand and foot and then solicitously ask, "How are you feeling, Honey?" That's when it happens. He looks at me like I am a complete idiot and finally manages to croak an answer, "I'm fine!" I want to yell at him and say, "The only thing that's fine is the line that I'm walking." He's using "fine" to shut me out and blip me off his screen.

Faced with change, particularly any change suggested by you, a man thinks, "Why should I have to change? There is nothing wrong with me." Everything is fine! He does not understand that you're not trying to change him; you're trying to find him and, yes, this will produce change. But, do not use that word with him. Instead, explain to him how you are trying to help him find his true self—that nice, sweet, caring, loving, wonderful human being who is underneath all those artificial layers imposed on him early on by family issues and being a male in our society. Oh, who am I kidding? He wouldn't understand a word of that. Just tell him you're trying to find the butterfly in his caterpillar. That will keep him quiet for a few minutes. Remember though, it is not your task to convince him there is something wrong with him. This would be wasting your time and his.

THE TESTOSTERONE TRIO

There are three characteristics of a man that need to be understood. First of all, a man wants "grown up" things like sex, marriage, and even kids. But, unfortunately, he wants to remain an adolescent when it comes to emotional maturity (or lack thereof). Your self-wellness and empowerment are no longer letting him remain in emotional puberty. Second, no matter how lousy his behavior, he wants to believe that you think he is perfect. This is why your earlier methods of blaming or criticizing him got you nowhere. Third, a man is a CIF (Crisis Intervention Feeler). He only allows himself to feel when the relationship is in crisis. In other words, when he sees he has finally pushed you to your limit, he lets himself feel just enough to be real sweet and loving towards you so you won't be mad anymore.

P.M.S. IN MARRIAGE

No matter how gentle you are, he may feel threatened, abandoned, engulfed, or otherwise frightened. In this case, he raises his "Back off! I am unapproachable" protective shell. He wants no one close physically, mentally, and certainly not emotionally. He lapses into full-blown P.M.S. (Problem Male Syndrome) and his Midol seems to come from ignoring, annoying, reproaching, and/or otherwise disturbing you. Possibly you reminded him of his mother, or he is suffering from a monthly case of methane retention, or his protective shell gives him cramps. Whatever triggers it, faced with human feelings, especially his feelings of neediness, your man will defend himself by retreating, or by becoming so weird and difficult you will pull away. (He probably prefers this modus operandi because it allows all the guilt to fall at your feet.) Either way, he has achieved his goal: enough distance between the two of you so he can raise his shield once again or at least retreat into his armored shell.

At the same time he fears being overwhelmed by "female" emotion, he also fears losing the warmth and comfort that you, as representative of the feminine, provide. Men collect experiences of rejection and abandonment, memories of being thrown out of emotional havens in which they felt safe and secure. Your partner may never have acknowledged these experiences to you or to himself, but this is why he is fearful every time the possibility of change occurs.

He may feel a little (or very) threatened by his fears, his feelings, and by you, and in response, he may turn on you at the most unexpected times. Particularly when everything seems to be going well, he will say or do something to indicate he has totally forgotten you are his friend, lover, and partner. Usually you have no idea why the temperature suddenly plummets below zero. So until the government requires men to wear estrogen patches, or it becomes legal to serve him Paxil House Coffee every morning, we women have to confront them head on.

The first few times this happened to me, days passed before I figured out what had actually gone down. Finally, I learned to be prepared and recognize the phenomenon within minutes of its occurrence. Please understand: this is a common problem in relationships. You are not alone. And you absolutely must stop this behavior! You must determine *now* that you will *never* again allow yourself to accept the role of target. Remember: Nobody can take your power from you without your permission. Once you decide to become empowered, you can catch his arrows in midflight and snap them like straws. You can learn when and how to make him back off, straighten up, and act right. Otherwise, you will relapse into old Surreal Love habits of putting yourself last and feeling badly about yourself. The most important lesson I learned is that by acting and reacting out of the emotionally healed level of Real Love, I could handle him and me anywhere, anytime.

Strategies for Living with Problem Male Syndrome (P.M.S.)

Problem Male Syndrome (P.M.S.) is hard to define. In a way it's like pornography. You don't really know how to describe it, but you know it when you see it. As you make headway in cracking his protective shell, you begin to feel genuinely loved and want intimacy. This wonderful feeling may be shared and may last a long time, but there is also the possibility, even the probability, that this warmth and coziness will bend him out of shape. Suddenly, without warning, he slides his armor back on and frequently, right before he yanks his head back in, he makes certain to push you safely away by doing or saying something that hits you right below the belt. Welcome to total and complete P.M.S.!

So what are you supposed to do now? It's easy! Always act from the Real Love of your own power! Do not be drawn into his! His P.M.S. is *his* problem. His behavior has absolutely nothing to do with you. Remember, you no longer believe your importance and wholeness come from your partner. You are no longer suffering loss of self due to Surreal Love.

Don't forget one of the most important things we talked about earlier. With men, "Nothing is fair in love and war!" They are too clueless to love and fight fair. Your job is to know when to put in the last word and then exit. Whether in the middle of a discussion, argument, party, or a visit to your parents—it does not matter. Whenever you feel he is lapsing into P.M.S., as calmly and politely as you can, state your position clearly and *walk*!

Go outside, to the store, another room, a museum, a bar, anywhere! Your man needs to learn that you no longer care if you embarrass or humiliate him by refusing to tolerate his acting out, or even if you embarrass yourself.

Your integrity and sanity must always be more important to you than being "socially appropriate."

SOMETIMES YOU'RE THE WINDSHIELD, SOMETIMES YOU'RE THE BUG

Most of the time, when I am out with my husband and our friends, he is a perfect "country gentleman" and I absolutely delight in being with him. I feel so good about him, us, and most importantly, me. There have been a few times, however, when, in front of other people, he has said something to me or acted towards me in typical P.M.S. clueless mode, and has sent me spinning back to "It must be my fault" surreal behavior.

Several years ago, we were at a restaurant with two other couples who were long-time friends. My husband was in an irritable state of P.M.S. He acted like everything I said or did got on his nerves. I had felt especially close to him prior to dinner and had no idea what was wrong. (He probably didn't either.) He was totally clueless about how his words and actions affected me. I retreated into my surreal-based behavior, letting him continue so I would not make anyone uncomfortable. But my self-esteem began to rapidly circle the drain.

Suddenly something clicked deep in my gut and yelled, "Enough already! Stop letting him affect how you feel about yourself." I had to make him pay attention. I looked him straight in the eyes and said, "Sometimes when I am with you, I don't feel very good about myself or you. Right now, I am concerned with me. I want to feel great about myself. Therefore, I am leaving. When you're ready to leave, you can call a cab."

The other couples sat open-mouthed. I apologized for any embarrassment the situation might have caused them. I asked them to understand, certain that they had also experienced difficult moments in their relationships. I assured them that my husband would graciously buy their dinners to compensate for any discomfort he and/or I might have caused. I then put on my coat, picked up my purse, left in my husband's car, and went to a movie. Destiny was on my side that night. The movie I chose was *Thelma and Louise*. This movie almost made me trade my husband's Oldsmobile for a convertible.

Now, I know some of you are thinking, Yeah, right, after fifteen years of being Docile Dolly Doormat, she was able to suddenly transform into the Unsinkable Molly Brown. Yes and no. Although the transformation was sudden and on the spot, the process of acquiring the strength to be ready for it had taken several years of internal growth, trying to develop Real Love for myself, then for Jim. For the first time in my relationship, I was emotionally healthy enough to act out of Real Love—for myself, for him, for what I and we deserve, and love for my friends and their desire to know the real, authentic me. My intuitive voice was finally loud enough for me to know what I needed to do in the moment.

Later I pieced together what had happened during that dinner. What finally made me get tired of being the "bug" and decide to be the "windshield?"

First, I paid attention to what my body was telling me. Each of his offhanded remarks had provoked small but vivid memories from the past which played like a videotape over and over in my head. The more they played, the more aware I became that I was getting a headache, my neck hurt, my stomach was upset, and my heart was beating faster and faster. I honestly acknowledged what I was feeling.

Second, I was honest with myself. I had to truthfully identify why I was feeling the way I was. Even though the truth hurt, it also set me free. The clearest message was that, although he had acted like a jerk, I had allowed and accepted his behavior. I was furious with *me*! I was angry at myself for my lifelong pattern of smiling politely even though my body was telling me I was hurting. I had been too insecure to make anyone uncomfortable. For the first time in my life, I knew with absolute certainty that I had to stand up for myself.

Third, I determined to listen to my body and to take action and get his attention. I acknowledged that continuing to be the "good girl" by suppressing my feelings would cause me to lose my physical and/or mental health. I thought with my heart instead of my head. I finally understood why the true definition of depression is "anger turned inward." I affirmed that I had the power within me to get my needs met. I did not "shut down" emotionally and withdraw. I confirmed that I must take action to create change. I made my announcement straight from my heart and left the restaurant.

As I drove to the movie on an adrenaline rush, I waited to feel anger, righteous indignation, or immense guilt. As I settled into the theater seat, however, I experienced deep feelings of warmth, safety, peace, and power. I knew I had created this for myself by retaining my dignity and standing up for what I knew was right. I internalized what I had learned from Emotional Healing and Achieving Self-Wellness.

- I acted for an ideal; I did not react against something.
- I acted consciously rather than lapse into unconsciousness.
- I cared deeply for me, him, and us; I was not apathetic.
- I chose survivorship over victimhood and did not lapse into grief.
- I felt strong and true to myself, unafraid of rejection.
- I felt empowered rather than angry and did not yell.
- I felt vital and able to act rather than paralyzed by fear.
- I chose to act from Real Love.

I felt a deep self-confidence I had never before experienced. For the first time in my life, I absolutely knew I could handle anything—in or out of my relationship, including the loss of it.

Never, ever, would I sacrifice my dignity again. I was beginning to really feel wholeness for the first time.

YOU CAN GO HOME AGAIN

Gifted with this knowledge, I found it easy to return home and deal with my now "shieldless," "helmetless" husband. I felt no trepidation whatsoever. I savored and nurtured my new feeling of integrity and did not let it slip away for one second. I knew my newfound, authentic voice had knocked my mate out of his P.M.S. and suspected he would move from shock to trauma as all his fears of rejection and abandonment arose. I also had the complete faith given to me by acting out of Real Love. What peace! This will always prevent you from arguing or having a heated discussion even when you are in a non-calm situation.

I knew I needed to give him reassurance. A man must learn to trust the fact that his partner is an ally, his best and closest friend. When it is your turn to provide your man reassurance, first stand beside him. Look in the same direction as he is so that he can begin to feel that you are "on his side." Then slowly turn towards him. Gently, but firmly, take his hands, look him straight in the eyes, and tell him you are on the same team. Remind him to never lose sight of your love for him. Ask him to trust and cherish forever your friendship, himself, you, and the relationship you have with each other.

Your love and reassurance will provide the safety net he needs to acknowledge his responsibility in the matter. That old line from *Love Story*, "Love means never having to say you're sorry," is a joke. Love means saying you're sorry an awful lot! Most men are basically nice guys who want to be loved. His apology may be clumsy, he may not truly understand why you feel the way you do, but he will be sorry for his words and/or actions that hurt you.

If your man refuses to take responsibility for the matter and either shuts you out or attempts to place all the blame on you, please refer to the appendix at the end of this book and get help fast. There can be a fine line between being clueless and being abusive. If you are unsure of which side you are standing on, seek help.

LEVELS OF RESPONSE TO YOUR PARTNER'S MISBEHAVIOR

We respond to our partner's clueless and crappy behavior depending on what level of healing we are in. For the first few years of our relationship, I was a "nonresponder" because I was unconscious. I was in Surreal Love with him mainly because of my old brain. I was so fractured and had so little concept of who I was that I did not even know enough about myself to recognize that his cluelessness impacted how I felt about myself.

Once I moved into apathy and grief (which for me seemed to arrive together), my response whenever my husband hurt my feelings was to hide in the shower and moan about how it was not the fault of poor, pitiful me. I became depressed and was stuck in apathy and grief for several years until the "blue robe" incident. Once I saw myself sitting on the bed asking him if my blue robe was the reason we seemed so distant, I woke up to knowing I had the power to heal myself.

Then fear set in. What if he does not like the newer, stronger me? If I change he may feel differently towards me. I wallowed in fear for a while, taking trips back to apathy and guilt and even unconsciousness until finally I got angry.

I was mad at myself and at him to the point that all I did was complain. I could not let go of being hacked off. I kept asking him, "How can you act this way?" "Why don't you pay more attention?" "How could you not know?" I kept berating myself with "Why do I let him treat me this way?" "Why do I let others treat me this way?" "What's wrong with me?" I was full of anger and I dumped a lot of it on him before realizing I could let it go. And guess what? I did! But remember, only after I allowed myself to feel the anger could I come close to letting go of it.

Once I released my anger, my heart hurt with the pain of loss, of hurtful words, of lost opportunity. I wanted to feel the soothing balm of completely letting go, of holding no grudges and feeling no blame, the balm only forgiveness provides. With grace, I learned to forgive (acknowledging the pain and releasing it) rather than deny (pretending it did not matter). During the last few years before the dinner incident, I had forgiven myself, and him, at least a million times. I had become so good at consciously letting go of hurt and letting forgiveness flow through me that acting and responding from Real Love began happening naturally. This was the most "freeing" feeling I have ever been gifted with.

PUT A MUZZLE ON IT!

The change was evident in incidents like this one. In the past, Jim had a tendency to "bark" orders when he got tired and "P.M.S.-y." This really drove the kids and me crazy. I use the term "bark" to describe an abrupt manner and tone of speaking. He was not harsh or loud or mean in any way. He would just leave out those little "niceties" that make us feel better. Instead of "Honey, could you turn off the light, please?" he would say "Turn off the light!" Or, if he thought our two boys were up too late at night (I definitely have two owls), instead of requesting they please go to bed, he would say, "Go to bed!" Needless to say, I did not like it, but none of my ploys to change the behavior worked until I was able to authentically respond from Real Love.

During the years I was unconscious, I did not even notice or hear his sharp tone. When I lived in apathy, I sometimes heard him, but I did not care. When I progressed into grief, I kept feeling sorry for myself because he spoke this way. As I moved into fear, I assumed I could not ask him to talk a little sweeter because I might upset him and then he would not love me. When I finally healed enough to be angry, I expressed it by getting mad at him. After releasing my anger and experiencing my pain, I was able to forgive him for not realizing how hurtful his tone could be and forgive myself for not being whole and strong enough to stop it. Now I was ready to act and respond from the Real Love I felt for myself, him, and our relationship. It was magic!

The second he started slipping into "barking" mode, instead of all those other reactions I used to feel, I felt empowered pleasure. Yes, weird as it sounds, that is what I felt. Because I was no longer blinded by fear, hurt, or anger, I could see how much I love being with him when he does not talk in that abrupt mode. I could feel how much I love the way I feel about me and the two of us when he talks nicely. I understood that he had learned that manner from his parents. For the first time in our eighteen years together, I realized this is not "just the way he is," it is just the way he knows. His parents loved him and they talked to him that way. How could he know his tone of voice might not sound so loving to us?

I got his attention by hugging him and kissing him on the forehead right in the middle of his "bark." In midsentence, he stopped talking and looked at me with a huge questioning look. I looked him in the eyes and told him how much I loved him. So that we could focus in the same direction and ease his comfort level, I looked at our boys. I got straight to the point and simply told him how good it made us feel when he talked a little nicer. It made us want to try to fulfill any requests he might have of his darling family. Then, to make sure he understood (remember, he's still a man), I gave him clear examples to try next time, such as "Sweet family of mine, Daddy's really tired. How about all of you tuck me in and then play a really quiet game, or maybe read? Thanks a bunch."

You know, guys can actually be pretty smart when they don't feel threatened, abandoned, or rejected. Daddy just nodded his head, sort of in a daze, and said, "Yeah, sure, uh, no problem." He now works very hard to remember to talk like the sweet person he really is. All of us are happier!

Getting to Forgiving and Real Love

Let me explain how I think this works. I really want to make it understandable because it's a process I have used many times to heal childhood and relationship wounds.

Step 1 – Make the decision that you will do anything it takes to stop being wounded.

You decide to heal. Instead of doing what I had always done, which was deny what I was feeling so I would not cause my husband or anyone else discomfort, you must let yourself feel your true emotions. When I sat in that restaurant chair, I silently asked myself over and over, "What am I feeling? What am I feeling?"

My mind, heart, and body integrated into one voice to answer me loud and clear: "You are angry. You are hurt!" Fortunately, I had finally acquired the self-respect and wisdom to hear and listen to my inner voice. I felt as if I were breathing for the first time. It is amazing how your soul responds when you reach for authenticity and realness!

It was easy for me to say what I had to say and then leave the restaurant. The other two women who were there called me later, first, to see if I was still alive, and then to ask me how I found such courage, such bravery, such audacity! The answer was easy. Strength and courage were not needed to leave the restaurant or even come home after the movie. The greatest courage of my life was needed when I allowed myself to feel my own pain. In doing this, however, I had to embrace step two.

Step 2 – Remember.

With that frozen smile on my face, I let the tapes of past incidents roll. I had never done this before and yet it felt so right. It seemed like viewing all those past images of times I had accepted being treated wrong took hours, but I'm sure it was just a few seconds. No one even noticed. I watched my inner tapes, felt my true emotions, and listened to myself.

Step 3 – Confess that you are responsible for your anger.

Once I embraced this concept, I recognized that only through my actions would I ever be able to release the anger and forgive myself for tolerating my husband's clueless behavior. After taking the action to speak out, leave, and go to a movie, I inadvertently moved to step four.

Step 4 – Get rid of anger, hostility, and pain through ritual.

Seeing the movie while eating popcorn was a ritual of release. Each time good ol' Thelma or Louise shot a bad guy, mouthed off at some obnoxious man, or blew up some sexist redneck's truck, I let go of my anger a little at a time. I pretended each handful of popcorn was a memory of being hurt and humiliated by a man. I chomped on each piece of anger (fortunately, no one was sitting near me). I chewed until I felt better and then washed away each mouthful of anger with a slug of Pepsi. By the time my two women heroes drove their convertible off the cliff, my pain went with them. It was beautiful! And it allowed me to let go of my anger before going home.

Step 5 – Forgive.

Concerning the restaurant scene, I was now ready for forgiveness. I had decided to heal, felt my true emotions, opened myself to remembering what had hurt me, confessed, taken action, and let go of my anger. Now it was time to forgive myself and then my partner. At this point in the process, I experienced forgiving both of us, and it was natural and freeing. As I drove home, I was smiling at how wonderful forgiveness was beginning to feel.

Forgiveness is not dependent on any action of the other person. It is the gift of grace that comes once you make the decision for your own healing, from the love within your heart. It is not something you can "think through." As with your other empowerment decisions, once you make the decision to forgive, you are already there. Once I decided to quit sitting in the restaurant with that stupid smile frozen on my face and decided to experience what I was really feeling, I took two very monumental steps in my life. I began to get well and I began to forgive myself and my husband. As a result, that night I experienced total peace for the first time in my life.

Step 6 – Invite the person who hurt you back into your heart and life.

I embraced the new, forgiving version of myself that would be present in my life from now on. Never would I let go of her again. I knew this with certainty. Now it was time to make peace with my husband.

(Please note that this is not a required step. It is possible to forgive without it. For example, if you have been abused, you may forgive the abuser so you can get on with your life without carrying the burden of hatred, judgments, and blame, but it may be very unwise to invite the abuser back into your life. For me, in this and many other circumstances, however, this was the right step.)

He was still in shock, as most men would be at this point. (You can always tell this because they have that "deer in the headlights" look.) The male feels pretty rotten about what he did and, in some form or fashion, will ask for your forgiveness. I always make sure that I let Jim know very clearly that whatever he decides at this point will not affect my love for him. It affects decisions I will face regarding our partnership, but does not influence my love. I will always love him. He may say things like, "I will try never to do that again," to which you respond, "Trying isn't doing; you never will do that again because I never will allow it to happen again."

Your man, who is a little sheepish and fearful at this point, will want to be forgiven. He wants everything to go back to "normal" as quickly as possible and will do almost anything to avoid confrontation. Men ask for forgiveness in many different ways. Some send flowers, others buy you new spark plugs, and some do nice little things they ordinarily would not think of doing. But I can pretty much guarantee that he's experiencing enough abandonment anxiety that he will try to seek your forgiveness in some way. He just wants everything to go back to that status quo as quickly as possible.

Ah, but here comes one of the hardest parts of Real Love. You must accept his apology and then let go of the hurt. In other words, you must assume the responsibility of moving forward. This is not an easy process, but it is the true path to healing and Real Love. As with your other empowerment decisions, once you've made the decision to begin to be healed, you're already there. Wellness will begin immediately!

When in a relationship with a man, you neutralize his behavior by ensuring that your self-esteem, self-confidence, and self-respect levels stay high. Only *you* can take care of yourself this way. Now that you know how to do this, you have the key to developing deeper intimacy and reigniting the romance in your relationship. Pick your battles wisely and let go of the behaviors that bother you but are not a big deal.

Hopefully, by this time, your man has opened his protective armor a little and maybe even kept his head out. But the odds are high he still holds a shield over his heart to protect himself from the vulnerability of loving you fully. Now that your man is learning your relationship is changing and beginning to see what Real Love is all about, it is time to teach him to come alive romantically.

12

Enabling Him to Make Love Longer Than He Can Go Shopping

WOMAN DISCOVERS THE REAL REASON MEN HAVE ERECTIONS

Yes, I'm afraid it's true. You know the honeymoon is definitely over when he can't last at shopping or making love for more than five minutes.

This is not news to you. But here's why men and women are so different: You have vivid, beautiful memories of the romantic times you and your mate had when you were falling madly in love with each other. You remember how sweet, kind, and gentle he was when you were together back then, before you became seriously involved or committed. When you ever so gently talk to him about these lovely memories, in hopes he might recapture some of that tenderness, does he look at you as if he has no clue as to what you are talking about? Well, it's true; he relates not at all to the man you remember so fondly. At this exact moment in time, a red-blooded man experiences a total break with reality. He has successfully transformed "romance" into "sex" and has no memory of life before this transformation. He truly doesn't recall being romantic and swears he has always believed foreplay is the number needed for a good poker game.

There are two simple ways to accomplishing more romance and closeness with your man:

> 1.) To get a man to want you, you must romance yourself first, and
>
> 2.) Know what motivates a man.

How Do I Love Me? Let Me Count the Ways

Women tend to have the almost overwhelming urge to respond to emotionally distant partners by withdrawing, over accommodating, and settling for less than what we really want. I made the mistake of doing more and more for my man hoping he eventually would be forced to show me how much he loved and appreciated me. Wrong! It is only when we start meeting our own needs that a man begins to notice. Until he sees how comfortable and happy you are being with yourself, he won't even know how much he wants to be with you.

As you build your relationship with yourself and focus on activities you love, he will begin to wonder, Who is this person living inside my partner that she wants to spend so much time with? What is it about her that is so interesting and so much fun? I thought she only wanted to be with me, but that is not what I'm seeing now. (This is a good sign. At least he has poked his head out enough to see.)

This change in the daily status quo may make your man insecure. After all, he is no longer the center of your universe and his fears of abandonment and rejection may get triggered big time. Make certain he understands that you are not planning to exit the relationship; you are simply developing your own interests. Do not even attempt to explain to him that you are learning to have Real Love for and nurture yourself, and this may cause the relationship dynamics to shift somewhat, but not to worry…Hello! He is clueless! This is way too deep for him right now. He will figure it out later, but he is incapable of this kind of depth in the beginning.

Reassure him by your actions. For example, offer to include him in your new passions. Ask him if he would like to drive you to the movie theater, the bowling alley, or the gym, so you can be with your girlfriends. See if he wants to pick you up and take you to dinner after your tango lesson—anything that includes him without overwhelming him. I know he "should" trust you, but he is a male. Change makes him fearful and paranoid. So, go easy on him.

Concentrate on your many positive attributes and on your right to have your needs met. Men can be pretty obtuse, but they will notice when you switch your focus of attention to your own needs instead of theirs. When you think about yourself and how terrific you are, you give yourself priority over him. He may not like it, but he will notice the increased value you are giving yourself. Blow all the dust off the self you have ignored for so long. Love this self and hold onto it for dear life, literally.

Now, consider some questions (and answers) about you. What is something you really want to do now for which you never seem to have the time? Do it! Find it! Want to be with you! Who are some family and friends you would love to see more often but have not found the time for? Find the time! Put yourself first. Want to be with you. Then, he will want to be with you too. (If he is lucky, you will find some time to fit him in!) Now, I know some of you are thinking that making time for yourself sounds like a great idea, but you are overloaded with school, kids, work, or whatever. Wake up! You must make yourself part of this load!

You cannot seek love of self through love of another. You cannot love yourself without finding yourself first. Love of yourself cannot be defined by what he does or does not do.

We women really want the whole mamma jamma, the open-armed, full-blown, knock-yourself-over type of Real Love. And that's what we deserve. To get it, we have to give it to ourselves first. The purpose of any relationship is to have another person with whom you can share your wholeness. So romance yourself. No one can keep you from being the person you want to be. In the words of my favorite soul man, James Brown, "Sometimes I feel so nice, I just want to kiss myself."

Make yourself a priority! Schedule time for yourself in the same way you schedule work, classes, dates, and doctor's appointments. An interesting thing happened when I finally did a "time diary" (Chapter 5) and started paying attention to meeting my own needs. I found, when I took the time to jog or go to a movie or practice the piano, the world did not stop revolving! My husband and children (once they picked their lower jaws up off the floor) simply assumed more responsibility. Responsibility they would have taken on years ago, but I would not hear of it. Please take the time and joy you deserve. Only then will the ones you love realize you deserve it.

Self-Romance Revvers

Arrange for your hubby or someone else to watch the kids, then pick one or more of the following:

1. Go to a movie by yourself. Throw nutritional caution to the wind and load up on popcorn, candy, and an ice-cold soft drink. Go a little early so you have plenty of time to go to the restroom, wait in the snack line, snuggle into the best seat, and watch all the previews.

2. Pick up a novel that you never seem to have time to read and take it with you to a nice restaurant. Savor every moment of having someone else cook and serve you while you relax, sip a glass of wine, and read your book.

3. Buy yourself a ticket to a play; art exhibit; symphony; dance, book, or poetry reading; or other event that you would love to attend. Thrill at having to consider no one else's opinion of the performance but your own.

4. Do any of the above, but with a good friend other than your partner.

5. Join a book club; take dance lessons; join a hiking, walking, or bicycling group. Just get involved in pursuits other than your marriage.

6. Plan a "girls' night out." Meet several of your closest friends at a nice restaurant (or even a trashy one). Make a toast to each other and to your friendship. Go club hoppin'. Laugh, dance, hug each other. It's these friends that will get your through the really tough times.

7. Check yourself into a hotel. It can be the Motel 6—or the Hilton. It doesn't matter. Just get a room with a queen size bed (yes, you are the queen for a day and night), a refrigerator or mini-bar, some sort of room service, and pay-per-view movies. This is how we recharge our batteries. I try to do this every couple of months or so. A hotel room becomes my "feng shui" sacred space, even if it's just for twenty-four hours.

8. Take a separate vacation. Take a few days and really savor a place that fits you to a tee. This could be going to the mountains, the beach, a monastery, a mall, some sort of retreat—go for it!

Whatever you choose, remember the three rules of self-romance:

1. Do not feel guilty.
(Your hubby and kids need their own time to screw up without you to fix things.)

2. You deserve a break today.
(You'll come back a much more loving wife and mommy.)

3. You can afford it.
(Think about it. Even though money is tight, somehow you find the money for the kids' soccer equipment, dance shoes, and Nintendo, and even for hubby's golf, fishing trip, and cable TV. Make yourself a priority!)

Partner-Romance Revvers

1. Have a weekly date night. Take turns deciding what to do. Enjoy being together, just the two of you, for a few hours each week. Go out to eat, on a picnic, for a walk, to the office and fool around, go bowling, play miniature golf. Just have fun!

2. Drop it! Let go of all the past crap he's put you through. Start fresh, right now. Begin making new memories. Discover each other all over again. After all, he's dating a new, wonderful, wild woman. Let the woman be fully present on your "dates."

3. Be passionate! No more little pecks on the check, little shoulder top hugs, or weak "love ya's." Come on, you empowered woman! Go the distance. At least once a day, kiss him like you really mean it. When you hug each other, make sure you give a full-blown, juicy, full-body bear hug (stiffness or tense hugging does not count). When he says "love ya," stop what you are doing, walk over to him, look him in the eyes, and say "I love you, too. I mean I really do love you!"

Enjoy the feelings this invokes.

4. Leave love notes, send cards, take him out to dinner, dance with him or for him, make him lemonade and cookies—do something a little extra, just for him, and just for the heck of it.

5. Notice him. When he comes home, stop for a minute and welcome him home. If he's home before you, acknowledge his presence in a loving way. Remember, you are healed and whole now. This will make you feel good, like you are giving him the precious gift of being loved by you.

6. Take vacations together. Make sure that at least one vacation, even if just for a weekend or one full night, is just for the two of you.

7. When you feel you and your man have finally developed Real Love, get married again. Jim and I went to Las Vegas to the Mission of the Bells chapel. It was great. The remarriage package included a limo with a bar and TV (I had to promptly confiscate the remote), the church service, minister, music, flowers, and champagne. It was perfect! All that was missing was an Elvis impersonator to give me away! We honeymooned at Caesar's Palace. The best part was that my ever-awakening husband planned every bit of this. A Real Love marriage, and honeymoon—aahh, life doesn't get much better than that.

The second key to having more romance and closeness with your man is to know what motivates a man.

MOTIVATING A MAN

Men are *not* motivated by wanting to have a better relationship. (I am assuming you have figured this out by now.) Men are motivated by three things:

1. **Fear** – of losing you first, of change second
2. **Greed** – for food first, money second
3. **Lust** – for you and for his toys (I am not sure about the order)

In other words, this goes back to my gentle metaphor of men sometimes being like cute pet puppies. A man would much rather roll around in the mud or dig holes in the yard than spend time making his relationship better.

THE CHALLENGE OF ROMANCE WITH THE ROMANTICALLY CHALLENGED

Most men are romantically challenged. This is absolutely no reflection on you. They have just never had to do this stuff before. A few men may love you more as you express your love for them, but your husband ain't likely to be one of them! I believe in the Blank Slate Theory, which assumes that men not only know nothing about true romance, but are new and unwilling students. You, however, are a creative teacher ready to accept the challenge.

If you have been in a relationship with a man for a long time, you may have repressed your romantic side. If this is the case, *reawaken*! Don't get drawn into his orbit. Several years ago, I slowly, but surely, noticed my hubby was not very romantic anymore. I don't mean "sex." I mean romance—flowers, holding hands across the restaurant table, moonlit walks, hugging, a wink across a crowded room. In other words, all those messages of desire, of intimacy, of love. The magic had gone out of our relationship and I had let it. I had been living and loving like a Stepford Wife with my entire relationship on autopilot. We looked great to everyone else. I made sure we took plenty of trips together, had weekly date nights, and celebrated all occasions appropriately. I made certain I went through all the motions of trying to have a perfect family and marriage.

My man was happy with this arrangement, and why not? I was carrying the entire relationship for both of us. All my loving attention was going to him. I did not feel chosen or wanted, but why should he notice? I did not give myself any attention, why should he? Worse yet, I had not even acknowledged my feelings to myself or to him.

To breathe new life into you, your man, and your relationship, you need to search deeply into your romantic core and ask yourself, "What will make me feel romantic, sexy, and in love when I'm with my man?" You must know what you want before you begin trying to teach your mate. All of us see other women with a man who does some little thing when they're together. He holds her hand, or puts his arm around her, or gives her a loving look and makes us yearn, even ache, to have a man do that for us. Be honest with yourself. Lose some of your inhibitions. Pay attention to what makes you feel good and then let him know. Get his attention! Do the unexpected. Totally disarm his sexual reserve. Have fun adding surprise to your life and his.

Sexy Romance Revvers

1. Rock the boat and seduce yourself first. Slide into clothes and undergarments that make *you* feel good and sexy. Wear things that you like to touch and feel against your body. Treat yourself to bubble baths, candles, a glass of wine. Wear thigh top stockings and enjoy touching yourself right above their tops. Stroke yourself. You may even forget he's there, but he'll remind you soon enough!

2. Rev up your fantasies. Read sexy "trash with class" novels. Rent movies with sex scenes that really turn you on. Anything from *The End of the Affair* to total trash (you know it's just for sex when the music is the worst you've ever heard).

3. Do unto yourself as you would have others do unto you. Do a little shopping in the ads in the back of *Cosmopolitan* or *Playgirl*. Buy some toys just for you, if you get my drift. I like to make Jim speechless by calling him at work and asking him point blank if he wants sex during his lunch break. If he can't get away, I start some phone sex, imitating a skit from *Saturday Night Live*. When he goes shopping with me sometimes, I put on a coat with nothing under it. I've never

seen a man take such a sudden interest in getting the shopping done. But you get the idea. Have fun!

4. Absence makes the heart grow fonder, as well as other parts of his anatomy. It can lead to seductive intrigue producing better sex another day. When you tell him "that you're not in the mood tonight, but would love to rattle the chandeliers tomorrow night," keep your word. He'll be loving the whole next day. The key is making "no" sound loving, sexy, and anticipatory. It salvages his ego and gives him a reason to be romantic for the next twenty-four hours. Men like challenges. Pleasure deferred can be pleasure enhanced if you work it sensitively and affectionately. This gives him a day to think about you and look forward to being with you.

5. Ask and you shall receive. Don't expect him to figure out what turns you on. You've got to tell him in plain English. Do you want more romance, kissing, being held, caressed? Tell him.

6. Put the giggles back in sex. Chase each other, have pillow fights, arm wrestle, play strip poker. Have sexy fun! Sometimes when Jim and I have date nights, I pack a pair of lacy thong panties in my purse. When I come back from the restroom (where I take them out of my purse), I discreetly hand them to him at the table or the movie. He's too turned on to figure it out, so I let him live his fantasy.

Talk about fun!

THE RITE OF INITIATION INTO ROMANCE

In the beginning you must initiate the romance (remember, we are talking romance, not sex). Whereas in Stepford Wife mode I created all the trappings of romance, in True Romance mode I learned to express my true feelings and entice my mate's participation. This may be difficult for some of you who have "any other man would have his hands all over me" personalities. And, it may be even more difficult if you feel uncomfortable with your body and lack confidence in your physical attraction. If you are still playing this negative tape, please go back to Chapter 1 and keep working until you look in the mirror and see the true beauty of yourself.

Your goal is to make your relationship more romantic for you. You have choices. You can grow older accepting your practical, unimaginative, nonamorous mate while you remain dissatisfied, or you could have an affair. But I think you really want more romance with the man you already have, or you would not be reading this book. So your third choice is to take charge of teaching True Romance to your partner. Get his attention and begin to act from a wholeness level of Real Love.

Begin by giving what you want. Take his hand, put his arm around you, kiss him on the cheek, sit in the back row at the movie and snuggle and smooch. Please try to be more discreet than my husband and I were. On one of our newly established weekly date nights, I decided to "go for broke." I purposely chose the movie, *My Best Friend's Wedding*, because I knew it would bore him to tears (no violence, action, or even R-rated sex). About halfway through the movie, I put the moves on my man and began necking. An elderly lady complained about our display of affection to one of the teenage ushers. When the young man followed up on her complaint, he was startled to discover two forty-something lovers in the back row. I died of embarrassment, but Jim loved it.

At the end of the day, do not wait for him to notice you are alive. Hug him and kiss him as if he were returning from battle (which he probably thinks he is). Ask him to carry you over the threshold, put on soft music and slow dance, neck, cop a feel, whatever. Take his hand and show him how to touch you, stroke you, and love you. Let down your defenses and do not be terrified of rejection. Be proud of yourself for showing him some of the things he could do to make you happier. Amaze him by being a little wild and crazy about him. Loving physically with enthusiasm really helps begin the process of waking up your man (as well as yourself)!

From Having Sex to Making Love

Showing him how to be romantic in the bedroom is a little more complicated. Once you become sexually involved with an adult male, he transforms romance into sex. He drops any pretense of making love and slides into the very nondemanding, nonvulnerable, nonpresent state of having sex.

When I first started teaching health promotion classes many years ago, a student wrote what I thought was a ridiculous answer to one of my test questions. Little did I know she had stumbled onto one of life's great truths. On their final exam, I asked students to explain the biological mechanisms by which the human penis becomes erect. This young woman wrote in very large letters that men become erect because they have a "penis bone." I incorrectly marked her answer completely wrong. At the time, I was too unenlightened to realize the poor girl must have had relationships only with clueless men. The existence of the penis bone is the only explanation for their ability to have sex with you without realizing you are present. The thighbone may be connected to the hipbone, but the penis bone is not connected to anything, especially not a man's heart or brain.

Now is the time for you to assume the responsibility of helping him connect his genitals to his heart and to his cute little head on those special occasions that you want him to actually make love to you and with you.

Honesty

To teach a man to make love to you, you must be willing to be totally honest with him. In other words, you may have to tell your obtuse darling something like, "I want to feel really wanted and loved. Be thinking of ways to make me really 'want it,' and we'll rock around the clock tomorrow night!"

You will have to stay prepared and in control of this delicate situation because, at this point, he will be lying there totally confused while his penis bone is rapidly withdrawing back into his abdominal cavity. Now, gently kiss him on the forehead, tell him how much you love him, and then tell him how much you'd love to snuggle. This will help him realize that you are not trying to be manipulative. You are honestly trying to be closer. He's going to need a night or two to come around so be sure to reassure him by hugging and holding him a lot even if he's pouting.

Putting your money where your mouth is

It's time to turn this dude on and put your "making love" plan into action. Carefully choose a night that you feel both of you stand a pretty good chance of feeling rather amorous. Starting at dinner, begin doing the little things that might excite him. Now you are probably thinking you should wear sexy negligees, garters, and black hose. Hollywood tells us this kind of stuff drives men wild and many women feel really sexy wearing these kind of things. We actually can make ourselves look pretty damn good with a beautiful Victoria's Secret ensemble. Yeah! Go, girl!

Hey, wait a minute. What was I thinking? The most romantic thing you might hear at this point from a guy is "Yeah, yeah—now take it off." And there you go again. Your planned romantic evening ends up being just about sex. Time to try a different approach. Even though I have an aversion to four-letter words like *cook*, *iron*, *dust*, and *wash*, the following scenario worked for me.

The quickest way to a man's heart, head, and sexuality is to play the domestic role to the hilt. He loves being made to feel he is the "Lord of the Castle." Come up with different ways to make him feel special. Use your imagination and have fun role-playing every now and then. (Note—if you're not actually role-playing, please read Chapter 1 again.) If you need ideas, use the lessons to be learned from having a beloved pet dog. Men love to be petted, be well-fed, have their tummies rubbed, be "scratched behind the ears," be kept warm, and be given lots of treats.

Forget the edible panties and wear the cutest little ol' apron you can find. What you do or don't wear under it is up to you, but you really should consider wearing the apron sans clothes. Serve him one of his favorite dinners without making him do the dishes. Hand him an ice-cold after-dinner drink and then ask to sit in his lap. Share the drink as you see fit. Just try not to dump it on his head if things don't go as planned.

Focus on connection

Your goal tonight is connection between you and him, not sex. Real love means connecting with each other. Focus on helping him realize he is with you, not just your body. Start helping him truly make love. Kiss him, hold him, snuggle with him. Do all the things that often get left out of sex. Be sure to look into his eyes and say his name. As things begin to heat up, do not lose the emotional connection. Flirt with him. It's fun to adore your man and let him know it. Tell him how much you appreciate the good things about him. Remind yourself that this is the guy who has stuck with you during bad hair days, grumpy moods, and no makeup. This is Real Love! Verbally and physically express your love for him, being sure to make periodic eye contact.

Some men actually will catch on the first time you try this approach and respond in kind. Others will need a few more tries to come around. Remember, for most of you, your guy really does love you. He simply does not spend much time thinking about it, and even less doing anything about it. His greatest fear is of losing you. He will never admit this but it is true. This is one of the traits of men. Remembering this basic fact should help you keep your confidence level high during the difficult times.

By the way, don't for a minute think that since he responded to making love one night, he will continue to do so in the future. He may try to return to silent, from the waist down, unemotional sex nearly every time. Enjoy that for what it's worth, but make your case on nights you want to make love. Just snuggle, stay cool, kind, and loving as you kiss him good night several times. This helps reassure him. Be willing to be content with a long snuggle if you can sense that tonight is a night he really does not have the energy to make love. As long as you are making your decision from the level of "love" and reaching out to him, you won't go wrong. You want to let him know, in as loving a way as possible, what your needs and desires are and that he is loved.

If he continues to remain clueless, then you may have to throw caution to the wind. I had to resort to using "props" to finally get my husband's attention. I am always amazed at how life sometimes presents us with glorious opportunities and perfect timing. One afternoon, a coworker gave me the heavy-duty responsibility of keeping a life-size blowup doll hidden until the weekend when we were having a surprise birthday party for one of the guys at the office.

That very evening, my husband wanted sex without even so much as a quick kiss. I know I have told you to be gentle and reassuring and still make him feel loved, and so on, but, on this particular occasion, I wanted loving and lost my temper when he refused. I stormed out of bed and, for the first time in our twelve years together, I went downstairs to the couch. Then I remembered the doll. I blew her up and put her in bed next to him.

He didn't notice I was gone until three in the morning, when one of our sons developed a fever and my husband tried to awaken "Party Patty" to find some Tylenol. When she would not wake up, he took care of the baby and wandered downstairs. He found me on the couch and, once he quit laughing, we made love until dawn.

If you search for and determine your romantic needs, give in to delicious abandonment, and don't give a flip about a rejected advance or two, you can have all the romance you want. Your man will learn to respond and eventually start taking a few initiatives on his own. When that happens, respond with all your heart!

THE WINE MAY BE MORE MATURE THAN YOUR MATE

A significant turning point for my relationship was Valentine's Day. For some men, a romantic holiday is the "kiss of death." Even hearing the word "Hallmark" can make the invisible shield go back up. My husband would reluctantly give me a card signed, "Love" every Valentine's Day. If I planned dinner out, he would take me. But, every year, he complained about the expectations of this day.

I finally wised up. I admitted that I couldn't get what I wanted on Valentine's Day so I changed my expectations. I hired a sitter, made myself a reservation at one of my favorite restaurants, took a terrific novel as my date, and left for my own evening out before hubby got home from work. I had a wonderful evening in two very different ways.

First, I found a way to never again give my very precious love and attention to anyone who did not make me feel wanted. Second, through a little detective work, my husband tracked me down as I was finishing my entree and a fine glass of Cabernet, which, unlike someone I know, had matured! We shared dessert, my dignity, mutual respect, and a true romance that has gotten only better. An added bonus was that it brought us closer to intimacy. And, yes, Real Love means having intimacy with each other.

Afterwards, I wrote a simple explanation for Jim as to how he could keep from screwing up future holidays. This is what I wrote:

Dear Handsome Husband,

True Intimacy is the Breath of a Marriage.

Every day - I would like hugs, kisses, snuggles at night.

Sunday - Make it a priority to be cheerful and smile nearly all day.

Evenings out - Do not walk ahead and leave me behind. Open doors and carry luggage—be a country gentleman.

On Mother's Day, Valentine's Day, Birthday, Christmas:
1. *Either take our sons shopping or spend time with them to make a card, write a note, and/or pick flowers.*
2. *You go shopping or write a 2-3 sentence nice note (any paper is fine) or buy or pick some flowers and attach a one sentence note (sentence must have a subject and a verb).*

Love,
Your Wonderful, Loving Wife

Enabling Him to Make Love Longer Than He Can Go Shopping ⌣ 225

Intimacy? How can you explain intimacy to a man? First, I gave my husband a card on Valentine's Day with the message that I no longer would keep my love for him within safe walls and boundaries. My ability to love was limitless. I asked him to someday give me the gift of sharing his inner soul with me so we could love each other with all our hearts. I don't think he understood a word I wrote, but at least I was able to plant a subconscious idea beneath his shield. This idea was the miracle of intimacy.

Intimacy is the ability to tell the truth about yourself and receive the truth about your partner, and still keep love alive during the process. Intimacy comes from one's heart and, therefore, should be the heart of every relationship. It's risky because your partner is a mirror. Until you hold yourself up to be seen by another person, you may never see some of your own weaknesses. This makes you vulnerable. Of course, through your partner's reflection, you can also discover your many assets.

If you have not gone through the steps of wholeness and are still operating from your old brain, you may wonder how someone who truly knows you could love you. When you are whole, however, you know that the more deeply someone knows you, the more they will love you. Intimacy entails having the courage to let your feelings show and to respond to that kind of openness in your partner.

THE FEMININE "DISDAIN" SYNDROME

A lot of men fear intimacy, or consider intimacy to be a feminine trait. And "real" men disdain anything considered "feminine." Men may have an overwhelming fear of losing the essence of who they are, or of being suffocated or engulfed. The stronger and more competent a man feels about himself, the less his fear of losing himself. We can help men learn that intimacy is safety, warmth, connectedness, and a trust that his well-being is in a safe container held by his partner.

Intimacy is having people in your life with whom you can openly and safely share your feelings, and know they will still love you and not hurt you with criticism, judgment, or rejection. Only then can you fully receive love and have an intimate relationship.

Intimacy allows you to lift your life to its highest potential. It's a glorious opportunity to decide and be who you really are. Relationships are our reason for being. From a relationship flows mental, emotional, and spiritual growth; communication; and mutual fulfillment. The real question in all relationships is not whether you won or lost in a particular situation, but whether you loved or failed to love.

THE TWO-MINUTE INTIMACY WORKOUT

When men are asked about their priorities in life, most list their marriage as the top priority. But like women, they do not schedule time for their priorities. Help him out with this. I told my husband I wanted two minutes (just two minutes!) every evening set aside for us to sit next to each other, hold hands, and talk only about us. These are two of the most intimate minutes of our whole relationship. Around 9:30 p.m. nearly every night, we have a chance to clear up any misunderstandings, plan a date night, or tell each other what we liked or did not like regarding something one of us said or did. Some nights we spend our time telling each other what we're grateful for and proud of in our marriage. There have been many times we talked way past the two minutes, but we never do less than that. Try it! There are very few men who would say they could not fit in two minutes for their lovely partner.

WHERE DO YOU STAND?

You may have to ask yourself some tough questions if your man refuses to respond to your loving, soul-felt advances. His attention, or lack thereof, reflects on you and your ability to love. You must ask, What parts of me do I love most—my compassion, enthusiasm for life, my ability to love? Then ask yourself, Am I able to live fully and express these qualities when I'm with my man? If the answer to this question is "no" or "not usually," then please observe and study all the relationships in your life. Pay attention to your friendships, your family, your relationships at work and other areas of your life. Also, look again at the possibility of creating new relationships, new friends, and new connections. Devote time and energy to the relationships that enable you to meet the needs of your soul while you live your life with your man.

As you follow the guidelines in this book, many aspects of you and your relationship will become clearer to you. Using this newly-found clarity and all your senses, you will be able to tune in to what your soul is trying to tell you. Recognize that your spirit, in its infinite wisdom, is aware of what you are feeling. If you are open to the message, your spirit will lead you to the right action.

13

Taking Him to the Limit One More Time

WIFE SHOWS HUSBAND BENEFITS OF GETTING ALL BENT OUT OF SHAPE!

Now that he is "more melted" towards Real Love, he actually stands a chance of getting out of his previously inflexible, monotonous surreal shape to become more expansive and have passionate Real Love. Stretching helps keep him open to giving you his attention and responding to your love.

The challenge here is to broaden his territory without provoking him beyond his comfort zone. Sometimes a man tends to live a very rigid, cautious life. Some are more uptight than others, but all men find great comfort and safety in the familiar and the known. Any sort of change in the dynamics of his life or yours is upsetting, even frightening, because he feels loss of control when change occurs. As a result, he rarely wants to do anything out of the ordinary. Also, doing anything outside of his daily routine might cause him to have to think about things. A man doesn't like to think when that thinking concerns his mate. This must change. Make him stretch. Stretching will broaden his "thinking" and "feeling" territory and will contribute to growth in your relationship. Assisting him in rearranging or supplementing parts of his familiar routine will help enable him to use his "new brain" to find new and different ways of seeing and feeling his value both to you and himself.

REAL LOVE STRETCHING

Warm ups:

Select an activity that you think might make him more aware of what makes a strong relationship. For example, look him in the eyes and tell him how very important it is to you that he go with you to the seminar on "Getting in Touch With Your Feminine Side." Explain how valuable his opinions and reactions to the seminar are to you. Then let him know that the only thing you want for your birthday, anniversary (remind him of the date), or whatever is that he take you to this seminar. By giving him your request as a gift from him, he may feel he has some control over this new situation—not to mention that he will be relieved of the burden of figuring out what to get you for a present.

Another way to try to accomplish relationship closeness is to take him to movies, concerts, plays, or performances that make him stretch his potential to see and feel what Real Love may be about. For example, I take Jim to movies such as *Life Is Beautiful, The Fisher King, Shrek, First Kiss, Ghost*—you get the idea. Going to plays like *Camelot* or *The Music Man* stretched his capacity to grasp some foundation of what Real Love might actually be about. As for music, my best stretching bit has been accomplished by a wonderful tradition in Asheville called "Shindig on the Green." Husbands, wives, and children all gather to play wonderful bluegrass and mountain music as families. You can feel their Real Love of their music and being together with every stroke of fiddle and guitar.

Stretch:

Now, let's make him stretch a bit further and a lot more vigorously. As alluded to earlier, it is very important to keep the KISS (Keep It Simple Sherlock) principle in mind. Always cut to the chase. What is it you really, really would like him to do that he may never have done before? Remember, male antennae can pick up thousands of stations, but he's probably only tuned to one or two—sports, food, or sex. Maybe you want to expand his territory to include going with you to your church group or a modern dance performance. Don't beat around the bush or try to approach the topic gently by telling him all the esoteric benefits of the arts. Simply get to the point. Tell him you want him to go with you to the New Age Dance Company performance because a nudity number has raised controversy and you really want his viewpoint. He won't remember much that you said except for "nudity number," but he will probably agree to go.

Never, ever expect him to feel like you do, act like you do, or even like to do what you like to do. Always choose his "stretching territory" very carefully. Decide what needs you have that are top priority for you and your relationship with him. Also, look at the things you want him to do with you and try to eliminate ones that might push him way past his comfort zone.

Or choose a different potion altogether. For example, even though I really thought it would help our relationship to go to a week-long "Getting the Love You Need" couples seminar, I knew asking Jim to stretch this far would pop the proverbial rubber band. A week-long, loving, touchy-feely seminar, although extremely important to me, would push him way past his comfort zone. So, I decided the best way to help him stretch toward being more loving was to start with tiny baby steps.

All I Want for Christmas is My Ten Love Lines

When he asked me what I wanted for Christmas, I sensed the perfect opportunity to make a significant, yet subtle, statement about our relationship. I proceeded gently, but firmly. I began by telling him what a truly wonderful man he was and how much I appreciated and loved all the gifts he had bestowed on me over the years. He had bought me absolutely everything I could ever need, want, or even think of desiring. Now, he's starting to get a little nervous that the present I'm going to ask for can't be bought at the closest shopping mall. He's right! I tell him I don't want him to spend any money on me. (His face was turning ashen.) I explain to him he doesn't even have to leave the house. (Now he is about to pass out!) I tell him I just want him to write down ten things he loves about me; that's all. That is the only present I truly want. (He is on death's door!)

He goes to the mall every day after work for two weeks. He desperately stands in the middle of the mall each day hoping, praying, that some store beckons him with a sign that says "Hand engraved plaques for that special someone—'Ten Reasons Why You Love Your Wife'—Get 'em while they last!" Much to his dismay, "the gift that keeps on giving" could not be bought. He was going to have to stretch, really stretch! He was going to have to sit down and seriously contemplate his love for me. This was tough, stressful, downright painful, but he did it and he lived through it. For Christmas I received ten beautiful sentiments on a piece of notebook paper which I will treasure forever. I know he simply cannot wait until next year!

Cool down:

The time has come to give your man another gift: surprise. Surprise combined with a loving partner always ends in pleasure. Surprise makes him have to stretch because he usually can't figure out what's going on. It teaches him that sometimes in life you should not bother to analyze. You just have fun!

- On a Monday Night Football night, leave him a basketful of snacks with a ribbon and a sweet note.
- Be really nice when he least expects it, like right after an argument.
- Bring him breakfast in bed.

- Slip a picture of you and a "Handsome Man" note under his pillow.

You get the idea. Surprise him with anything you do not ordinarily do, being sure that you don't push him out of his comfort zone. For example, the typical man would rather dig a hole to China than have the waiters at Golden Palace bang the gong and sing "Happy Birthday" at his table.

Surprise keeps a man from going back to that rigid routine of his and teaches him flexibility. Who knows, maybe after awhile (probably a long while), he will discern that you might enjoy a surprise from him. I love surprising my husband with what I call little "flirt notes." I grab a Post-it and write about how cute he is and put one in his lunch, on the windshield, or on his pillow. He actually caught on. He began surprising me, leaving "lovey-dovey" messages on my answering machine at my office. He figured this out all by himself! To be happy with your man, he must stretch many different ways. Help him find what makes him happy. With your gentle encouragement, you will be doing both him and you a tremendous favor.

Sometimes the Stretch Must Look Like a Man, Smell Like a Man, and Walk Like a Man

A note of caution: To be a "man" in our society requires a lot more than just going through puberty. They have to be tough, strong, the provider, the protector, the athlete, and so much more. For your man to enjoy having fun and being human as he stretches, he must see himself, and believe always that his peers see him, as a "Man." So, be cognizant of the fact that when a "stretch" might threaten his manhood by making him feel vulnerable, you need to move slowly. Back up, take baby steps, and show lots of love and compassion. Some men are very secure in their manhood, but most men are not in that group.

I learned this pretty quickly during my first attempt at getting Hubby to start stretching. I was so thrilled to learn he wanted to make homemade bread to expand his repertoire of experiences in life. For months our home smelled absolutely wonderful. I loved seeing him with flour on his chin and hearing him talk about the different ingredients he used in his breads. I found his stint as a bread maker extremely appealing and sexy. He did not! There just was not enough machismo in making bread for him to deal with the stress of keeping his starter alive. I swear, the man needed a crisis hot line the last time his starter died. When he buried it in our son's goldfish graveyard, I knew the smell of bread in my kitchen was forever gone!

His next attempt at stretching smelled almost as good. He became a cappuccino maker. Every evening he presented me with a frothy concoction to delight my palate. I was totally in love. I looked at him with adoring eyes as I enjoyed every sip. But, alas, this too was not manly enough to keep him motivated. After two months, his beautiful coffee machine began gathering dust.

All right, time for a machometer reading. The best way to ensure that your man keeps his shield off is to enable him to stretch to his bliss (i.e., something that makes him happy, content, and lose track of time). Maybe he has always loved model trains, remote control airplanes, or fly-fishing. Maybe he doesn't even remember, or know, what he enjoys. Help him find it. Encourage him to find, or make time for, a hobby or project he truly loves. He will be much easier to live with (particularly when he retires) and this will give you time and energy to pursue your passions. Maybe you could pick a passion or two you can pursue together. Hopefully, he will find something he likes that you can live with.

Slowly, I came to recognize that mine was going to have to choose something that made him feel like John Wayne. By teaching him all I have discussed in this book, I have helped him find in himself his sweetness, softness, and even his vulnerability. I have caused him to know that, in my eyes, he is most manly when he is gentle and kind and emotionally available. But, to find his bliss, I realized it was equally important for him to find something that made him manly in his and other men's eyes.

He chose target shooting and went to the extreme. I despise guns and now I'm living with the "Lone Ranger." But he is so happy down on the range and that makes me happy and us happy as a couple. When you have coached a man to spend time for himself doing something that may help him get in touch with "the little boy who longs to play," you probably will find that, when he comes home, he is a lot more pleasant to be around. He is likely to be more open and available for you. Now, I know exactly what you're thinking. You're wondering how in the world did helping him find the bliss of the Defensive Handgun Training Academy bring us emotionally closer in our relationship? Well, it's called having a more contented partner and gaining leverage or bargaining power. When your man finally stretches to something he loves, then he will do or agree to almost anything to keep his hobby and his peace with you.

The only time in our entire married life my husband was willing to attend counseling was before he left for seven days at the Advanced Handgun Training Academy. I told him I would gladly agree to give up a vacation together as long as he would sign up for Relationship Training Academy (counseling, of course) the following week. When he returned with his new handgun skills, I had a list of fifteen possible counseling dates from which he could select five. He did. That's how stretching and finding his bliss made us closer than we had ever been.

You will see it, too. He becomes more open to being attentive to what is important to you. He is approachable so much more often. Savor these moments of togetherness. Express love, be vulnerable, get mushy. Bask in this wonderful feeling of truly liking being with him.

DO NOT LOSE SIGHT OF YOUR BLISS

In some relationships, the man has already found his bliss and gone way overboard. The kind of guy I'm talking about is the one who lives and breathes his bliss. He is the fisherman, golfer, hunter, trail biker, jogger, whatever who seems to follow his passion while everyone and everything else gets ignored. You know the type. I call these men the "Bubbas" of the world. If Bubba likes to fish, he not only goes fishing anytime he is not at work, he also talks about fishing incessantly, wears fishing clothes, and buys more fishing toys. It's enough to make you tear your hair out!

Women! We must learn from the Bubbas! Do not waste your energy being mad; instead observe, stand firm, and make it win-win.

Observe

Bubba is a master at knowing and setting his priorities. To be quite honest, I am jealous of his ability to push anything and anybody to the wayside in order to follow his bliss. He does this by assuming that you will automatically carry most of life's load. Observe his actions and yours. Are you taking care of the house, kids, relationship, and everything else while he goes off to play? Do you want some time to play, too? Of course you do. Do you want some time together to actually have a relationship? Yes! Now do it!

Stand firm

To stand firm, you must know what your priorities are and exactly what it is you want. If you want one day of the weekend to follow some of your own passions, firmly tell Bubba he can go fishing on Sunday, but you will be gone on Saturday. Then you may have to explain his options. (Remember, no more than two.) Clearly tell him that he can take the children fishing with him on Saturday or he can stay with them at home. Do not deviate from or complicate your message. Use what you learned in the "attention" chapter.

Make it win-win

Make your relationship win-win! Negotiate, bargain, stand firm, do whatever it takes for both of you to get your needs met. You need as much time to meet your priorities as he does to meet his.

He won't make the choice on his own to behave in a different way. Use what you have learned in this book to enable him to choose to have a better relationship and to help you meet your needs. In other words, criticizing, complaining, and punishing will never work. But getting his attention and rewarding him makes him happy enough to act better.

One of the best ways to help make your relationship more win-win is to think of fun, innovative ways to sometimes participate in each other's bliss. I call this Relationship P.T. (Participate and Trade). For example, I don't like guns. But I love my husband. I love that he has found his bliss, and I love being with him. Some of the best times we have are when I pack a picnic lunch and ride with him to one of the target ranges. This gives us a glorious opportunity to be together. We enjoy at least a couple of hours in the car just talking, laughing, and listening to music. We have a wonderful picnic out in the country and I just rest and relax while he goes off to play. We both have a great time.

The even sweeter result that participation often brings is a glorious trade. Last weekend my big ole dude said that if I would give him the pleasure of my company at a regional shooting competition, he would agree to take dance lessons. My man never ceases to amaze me! I can bask in the full reward of the hard work of bringing myself and him into Real Love. We are two human beings in an intimate, growing relationship. Of course, I still occasionally revert to my insecure mode and he revisits obnoxiousness, and I have to reread my basic training manual again. But the times in between, the times of living from Real Love, are longer and more beautiful.

REAL LOVE GRADUATION EXAM

All right, time for your final graduation exam. Write down five words that describe you at this very moment.

Here are five words I wish for you:

E = Enthusiastic
A = Adventurous
R = Real Love
T = Together
H = Humorous

Enthusiastic—Yes! You are enthusiastic about life, love, yourself, and your partner. You have found new and renewed vital energy sources that give you a zest and passion for living even during life's most difficult days.

Adventurous—By reading and applying even just a few parts of this book, you have experienced a journey of emotional upheaval, growth, risk, and excitement. You are the most remarkable adventurer! The courage you have shown yourself and your man is unprecedented. The benefits of all you have done will continue to reward you and your relationships on a daily basis.

Real Love—You have Real Love. You are honest, real, wise, and respectful of yourself. What a gift for you and your partner. As you continue to learn ways to cherish yourself and thrive as a self-well woman, your love will grow more strong and beautiful with each new sunrise.

Together—You have got it together, girl! You have been putting the pieces of you and your life into your incredible, gorgeous self! Your life and your relationship may still be in utter chaos, but now that you are a self-well woman, you have the control to pull it together. Because of your Real Love togetherness, you and your man can have a wonderful connectedness as individuals, partners, and human beings.

Humorous—To get through this book, you had to laugh at yourself. God knows you had to laugh at your man. I've always been taught that it's impolite to laugh "at" someone, but I don't agree. When I could finally laugh "at" me and Jim, I knew I was healing. I knew our relationship could make it. I could feel us growing into Real Love. Your mission is accomplished. Mission Seemingly Impossible has become Mission Possible, and it happened all because of you. You have graduated from Surreal Love to Real Love. You are grounded in self-wellness and wholeness. You are consciously and beautifully human. You have taken the lead and led yourself and your man to commitment to living together. Through your wholeness, you both will feel beautifully grounded as you nourish yourselves with the life energy that flows from your home of Real Love. Welcome home. There truly is no place like it.

You have a committed home in each other now. What should this new home feel like and be like? Now that you've finished this book, you should feel the following at least once a week with your man:

Joy—He should feel good for you now and bring more joy than pain into your life. Your relationship with him should feel very nourishing rather than toxic.

Comforted—You should enjoy doing a few things with him or talking to him in a way that makes you feel fulfilled, happy, and at peace.

Energetic—Having moments of joy with your partner energizes and excites you.

Inward Glow—He makes you giggle and vice versa. Being able to laugh with each other always makes your inner light shine.

Compassionate—Your heart should feel more full and open to others. You want to reach out and give to others.

Positive—You should have a different perspective and a higher threshold for becoming anxious, worried, or irritated with your man.

Real Love—You want the best for him and want to spend time with him. You experience adoration, fondness, kindness, passion, tenderness, and attraction. You want to touch, hug, or hold him. You are now open to trusting him, seeing his positive side, and feeling safe.

Better—Holding onto Real Love promotes wellness.

Enjoy every minute!
Love,
Cheryl

14

One Day at a Time, Sweet Jesus

Loving a man can be difficult. When he is being a jerk and in full-blown P.M.S., it is nearly impossible. Commit to one day at a time. Otherwise, it can be overwhelming. Nurturing a man to a fully human state is much harder than raising a child. Sometimes it is painful to watch as he takes his baby steps or, as in the case of my husband, crawls toward authenticity and learning to truly be present in our relationship.

Your man is so very blessed to have you as his mate. By following some of the suggestions in these chapters, you have been willing to "put your butt on the line" for the relationship. You have stood strongly for what is best for him, while first standing for what is best for you. You have used a winning combination of humor, surprise, and self-validation to help him open up, let you in, and begin to *feel* what it's like to be a human being.

I am not Hillary Clinton or Tammy Wynette. I will not stand by my man because he is president or even if it will give me a hit record (well, maybe if it will give me a hit record). I am a great partner, however, and I will stand by my man one hundred percent when I feel that I am loved, respected, and cherished, and can be who I really am. Most of us sincerely love our partners and want to stay in a relationship with them, but not if it means sacrificing our wholeness and, therefore, our happiness. If you stay with your man but remain blind and deaf to the things he does to chip away at your personal truths, beliefs, integrity, and self-esteem, not only do you fail your relationship, but you fail yourself.

Some of you may feel you already have reached a fork in the road in your relationship. Consider the possibility that the decision is not whether to stay or leave. Let the only decision be taking the road to wholeness. One of the greatest, most glorious moments in your life is the moment when you stop being afraid. No more trying to live up or down to someone else's expectations of who you should be. No more wasted energy trying to behave in a way that makes everyone else happy. You must make yourself happy. You must love and cherish *yourself*. As long as your primary purpose in living and loving is to be true to yourself, to your soul, then your relationship decisions will be easy. You'll always be able to hear the answer in your heart.

I hope this book has helped you search for ways to feel more loved by yourself and your man. I hope you feel more deeply recognized for who you are. Learning to feel love by its presence, rather than its absence, should begin to feel natural as your man slowly removes his shields. I feel confident that, after putting this book into action, most of you will find you are with a man who hears his "wake-up call." Be patient. For some men it takes a lot longer than for others. As long as you always validate you in your relationship, you will never get lost in the quest to be in a relationship with a man who truly is alive and authentically human.

Now, put the book down and close your eyes. In your newly self-validated and empowered state, think of three or four characteristics of your man that attracted you in the beginning. Visualize him acting in the sweet and caring way you know he can. Plant these lovely images deeply in your brain and nurture them. Call them up from time to time and they will help strengthen the loving feelings you're having for your partner. He will have no choice but to be moved by all this positive energy that is flowing from you. Once again, you are changing the dynamics by not allowing negativity to be the focus of your relating.

Expect that there will be times when you will have to make him pay attention, ward off his P.M.S., remind him how to be romantic, heal wounds, and make him stretch. But, now that you are more in touch with your core being and are connecting with your man on a positive level, these occasions will be less and less frequent.

We women can all relate to the old adage, "Men…you can't live with them, and you can't live without them." I hope, after reading this book, you will be able to say that you actually take delight in being with your man.

ME AND MY MAN: AN UPDATE

Let me fill you in on how things are going with me. It's very late at night and I am very upset with Jim. He's at his computer and I tell him I need to talk. He turns, looks at me, and smiles. He is so handsome! I begin talking about a very important problem we have been having. He pulls his chair closer to mine so we are close and facing each other. He is so caring! As I continue talking, my heart hurts and I get teary-eyed. He unplugs the phone. He is so attentive! I finish what I need to say. He responds and gently explains how the misunderstanding and confusion occurred. He is so loving! He says he's sorry and he understands why I was hurting. He is my hero! I tell him I love him and start to walk away. He rises from his chair to hug me and hold me. He is such a beautiful man. He is so human!

This year for Christmas, he gave me a gift of love and surprise and he did it all by himself. He checked my schedule to be certain when I was off, made a three-day reservation at a beautiful romantic inn in the North Carolina mountains, and even found baby-sitters to come stay with the boys at our home. I tell you, he gets plenty of "atta boys" for this one.

WHERE DO WE GO FROM HERE?

We are not asking our men to be more emotional. We are asking them to be more responsive and more emotionally available to us and even to other men. We are not expecting too much in asking this.

Our goal, as individuals, should be to always connect with the life-giving parts of both femaleness and maleness. Society must begin to drop the male and female labels we continue to apply to totally human attributes of both men and women. In other words, why should a woman be considered "manly" if she is strong and businesslike? Why should a man be thought of as "feminine" when he is kind and gentle? As a culture, we must learn to lovingly accept and support the fact that even though men and women are different, each is a whole person striving to connect with all the positive traits of being authentically human. Then, we, as individuals, as couples, as nations, stand a real chance of living decently and with integrity united on the same planet.

I hope your journey has helped you discover and create more love in your life than you have ever had before. I hope both you and your man have connected on levels you never dared to think possible. I hope each of you has come to the life-giving revelation that winning or losing is not the test. The real test is loving or failing to love.

The truth is relentless. Now that you have opened up the windows of your soul, it will always guide you to what is true. Have a blessed, glorious life rich in love and meaningful relationships. And always remember the message of your heart: "There is only so much you can understand. The rest is meant to be felt."

CLASS DISCUSSION: JUST A BIT MORE

Below you'll find some questions I am often asked and my answers to them. You may find that you have similar concerns in your own relationship.

I feel like I have no control in my relationship with my husband. He is constantly reminding me that, as he puts it, since he makes the money, he runs the show. I don't know how to respond to this.

You are asking me how to respond to his statement? The answer is—don't. Don't waste your time trying to figure out an answer to that kind of intimidation. It's time for you to start "doing." You are mistakenly assuming that money equals power. This is what he wants you to assume. But now you know better.

You have the real power in your relationship. You are the woman. You have control because you have the power to change. You will learn to become whole and secure in who you are. You will nurture and develop Real Love for yourself. You will become confident enough to do what is best for you in your relationship and this will be best for both of you. As you gain control of *you*, you change the dynamics of your entire relationship.

To me, men are like room service. I have real love for both of them; therefore, I need them. Just like my man, hotel room service adds excitement and richness to my life. I have never seen where room service really comes from. As far as I know, it comes from another planet. But it is totally within my control to have it. I just need to know what I want, how I like it, and how to dial for it. Real Love is also up to me. I need to know and understand my needs and call up the strength and love I know I have to get what I want in life. I have the control I need to start a journey towards Real Love and commitment. You will, too.

Dr. McClary, I've tried so many times to get my husband to be more open with me and not shut me out. He will never talk about his feelings. It just seems hopeless.

Most men are clueless when it comes to emotional intimacy and love in a relationship, but they truly are not hopeless. Men often find self-disclosure very threatening; showing one's softer side is not considered masculine. Many otherwise "successful" men are emotionally impoverished. They have not yet caught up with women in terms of personal growth, knowing how to work on a relationship, or knowing how to be a good friend.

But things are changing. You may understandably be asking yourself: If all men are difficult, are you doomed to be unhappy? Does it mean you have to choose between swallowing your anger or nagging your partner for the rest of your life together? No. Change can happen. Difficult men can get better. However, the only way that change will ever happen is if you take the first steps.

You are men's hope! You can save men from themselves! Guide men to accept their own nurturing sides and embrace all emotional realms of themselves yet still be able to feel masculine. Show men how to enjoy intimacy without feeling threatened and controlled. Teach mankind how to be kind men, or even better, to be compassionate human beings. Women and men both have an innate and equal ability to engage in the full range of human experiences.

Be confident. Confident women keep their men. And when you get discouraged, try not to see men as jerks. Please look deeper. They really do want Real Love as much as you do. Men are not hopeless. They have women. As a woman you will become strong and whole enough to gain and use what you learned in the book to connect with him at a level of Real Love. You'll have a great time. So will he!

If you are unhappy—I mean really unhappy—with your relationship, wouldn't it be easier and better for all concerned to just get a divorce?

I'll first answer your question as an attorney. No. Divorce should be the last resort (unless, of course, it is an abusive relationship). No matter what the alimony, settlement, or custody arrangement, nobody wins. Any so-called "victory" is a hollow one. I despise divorce law. It brings out the worst in couples and even takes them to new lows.

To answer your question as a women's health professor, I'll say the same thing. No—divorce is never easier. Of course, if children are involved, the toll on the family is often irreparable. But the other huge and very common problem is that unless you go ahead and do the soul work necessary to become whole, you'll just have the same types of problems you had the last time you were married, but with a different man. If you don't work through your issues, they will be right there with you no matter how many times you marry.

Dr. McClary, my father left us when I was seven years old. My mother did fine without him. I just don't believe women even need men in their lives. Why bother trying to have a committed relationship?

For several years, I too went through an "I am Woman, don't come to the door" stage. I didn't want or need a relationship. And after Ken, I was pretty much convinced they were all jerks. Then along came Allen and eventually Jim, and I found myself in an "I am Woman, hear me snore" phase. I was so bored with men. Allen's inability to question or challenge anything about our relationship bored me to unimpressive tears. Whereas, with Jim, my husband, I felt stuck and bored several years into our marriage. We had a family; we were comfortable. But him being on the couch with the remote or on the computer with the mouse left me feeling pretty stuck and miserable. I felt like your mom probably felt—Who needs this crap anyway?

But remember when I said I was crying in the shower at night? Well, I think I was crying for "I am Woman, give me more!" I liked having children and a husband. I wanted to stay committed. But I couldn't do it with the lousy sort of Surreal Love we had at the time. I had lived long enough and hard enough to know what all three of these stages (don't need a man, bored with a man, and wanting a different man) felt like. I had been through the pain, anxiety, uncertainty, depression, and part-time peace and comfort that each of these three existences bring. And that is all they are—existences. I was just going through the day-to-day motions of living. Yes, I was alive, but I didn't have much life. It was okay. I got along just fine. But it wasn't enough for me. I deserved better!

Our need for relationships is at the core of our being, and a relationship with a man will give you a remarkable opportunity to explore, discover, and decide **who you really are**.

Of all the verbiage I've laid on you, the above four words are the real key to answering your question. Until you put the focus on you, *nothing* will change, especially you! Learn from and use your relationship with your man to find *you*. As you learn how to find Real Love with him, you will feel fulfilled and enriched. The reason you have a relationship is not only to find yourself, but become yourself. For so many of us, men are our wake-up call to our souls. Embrace this, love it, and you will begin the journey home to your self.

How? The baggage you are carrying around in your soul because of your father is a heavy load. It's pervasive in your friendships, your life decisions, your family dynamics, and I even heard it in the way you asked me your question. As you progress to cherishing yourself, unpacking your emotional baggage, and growing towards wholeness, you will be using your new, rational brain much more often. This holistic thinking will amaze you. You will never again ask, "Do I need a man?" Instead your question will always be, "What does my heart feel would be the most loving action I could take for myself?" The rest will follow.

Whenever I ask my husband if he loves me, he always answers, "I married you, didn't I?" Why does this bother me so much and make me feel not very loved? I mean, he says it with a smile on his face and he says it in a nice way. I know he loves me, but it still feels weird. Oh, I don't know. I can't explain it.

Oh yes, you can. You've done a beautiful job of explaining it. Where you need just a little help is in actually listening to all that you are saying. Your husband's answer is evasive. You are taking it personally, but it has nothing to do with you. His vagueness is his "old brain" trying to feel safe and less vulnerable by keeping you insecure and guessing. This gives him control.

For you to take the lead, first of all do not take his elusive answer personally. Stay on track and get his attention by saying something similar to, "I must not have asked my question clearly enough. What I really want to hear is that you love me very much." This should get the answer you really want.

Also take note that most men really do believe that because they married you, this means they love you. They are honestly puzzled that you even have to ask. They don't grasp that commitment is like skin. It's soft, flexible, breathable, and continually renewing itself with new growth. This is probably too much for him to understand, so just remind him that when he tells you how much he loves you, it makes you feel like you did on your wedding day.

Why do women always have to be the ones to "fix" the relationship?

Because women are the ones who want to fix it. Men don't see that it's broken. They think the relationship is fine. Quality isn't an issue to them. Even though you're leaving "grenades" all over the place, warning him the marriage is about to blow up, he can't fix what he doesn't see is broken.

Here's how I understand it. I imagine for a moment that I am perfectly happy and content with my marriage. Then one day my husband comes home and says, "Cheryl, I'm not very happy in this relationship. I feel that it would really help us if you would also learn to crawl under the car and change the oil and then climb to the second story of the house and clean out all the gutters."

I would react to this request with a resounding "Hell, no!" First of all, his request would make absolutely no sense to me. I would be totally clueless as to what any of this would have to do with our relationship. Secondly, I do not want to do either of these things. So I wouldn't.

One of the things I'm trying to explain in this book is that this is how our requests concerning "fixing" the relationship come across to most men. It just makes no sense to them. They don't get the connection. So what I'm saying is that we have to be whole enough to let go of trying to expect men to "fix it." We simply become self-loving enough to change our behaviors to get the desired response we want from our partner so that both of us can be happy.

For example, if Jim really wants me to help change the oil and clean the gutters, he would do what I've taught you to do in this book: He would get my attention slowly and calmly by bringing me an ice-cold Dr. Pepper and some freshly popped popcorn when I'm just finishing up grading exams for class the next day.

He pulls up a chair directly across from me and gently asks me to please help change the oil and clean the gutters sometime on Saturday. He wipes his brow as he finishes his request. He holds my hand when he sees I have no clue what he's talking about. He would smile and tell me how much he is looking forward to us getting all grimy together under the car and how much better he feels knowing that we will clean the gutters as a team. He stresses the "together" and the "team" part.

Then with a sly grin, he passes me a note. It says:

Thank you, honey, for loving me enough to be my partner in taking care of our car and our beautiful home. When we finish our work on Saturday, let's celebrate together with champagne in the shower. You are gorgeous.

I love you, Jim

What would my response be?

"Hot damn! How many days 'til Saturday?"

Bibliography

Boston Women's Health Collective. *Our Bodies, Ourselves.* New York: Simon & Schuster, 1998.

Firestone, Robert and Joyce Catlett. *Fear of Intimacy.* Washington: American Psychological Association, 2000.

Good, Nancy. *How to Live with the Difficult Man You Love.* New York: St. Martin's Press, 1994.

Hendrix, Harville. *Getting the Love You Want.* New York: Harper Perennial, 1990.

Karbo, Karen. *Generation Ex.* London: Bloomsbury Publishing, 2001.

Kidd, Sue Monk. *The Dance of the Dissident Daughter.* New York: Harper Collins Publishers, 1996.

Kolbenschlag, Madonna. *Kiss Sleeping Beauty Good-Bye.* San Francisco: Harper and Row, 1979.

Kushner, Harold S. *How Good Do We Have to Be?* Canada: Little, Brown & Co., 1996.

Northrup, Christiane. *Women's Bodies, Women's Wisdom.* Potomac: Phillips Publishing, October 1999.

Shaevitz, Marjorie. *The Confident Woman.* New York: Harmony Books, 1999.

Sills, Judith. A Fine Romance. New York: Ballantine Books, 1987.

Tannen, Deborah. *That's Not What I Meant.* New York: William Morrow, 1996.

Walsch, Neale Donald. *Conversations with God.* New York: G.P. Putnam's Sons, 1996.

Waterhouse, Debra. *Why Women Need Chocolate.* New York: Hyperion Publishers, 1995.

Resources

This is a listing of some of the books I have found helpful in my journey towards Real Love. It is by no means a complete compilation. There are hundreds, maybe thousands, of other excellent resource books in this same subject area, but this list will help you get started.

ABUSIVE RELATIONSHIPS

Ackerman, Robert J. *Before It's Too Late: Help for Women in Controlling or Abusive Relationships.* Health Communications, Inc., 1995.

Bass, Ellen, and Laura Davis. *Beginning to Heal: A First Book for Women Survivors of Child Sexual Abuse.* Harper Collins, 1992.

Berry, Dawn Bradley. *The Domestic Violence Sourcebook.* Lowell House, 1995.

Evans, Patricia. *The Verbally Abusive Relationship.* Adams Media Corporation, 1996.

Hamberger, L. Kevin, and Claire Renzetti, eds. *Domestic Partner Abuse.* Springer Publishing Company, 1996.

Hegstron, Paul. *Angry Men and the Women Who Love Them: Breaking the Cycle of Physical and Emotional Abuse.* Becon Hill Press, 1995.

Jantz, Gregory L. *Healing the Scars of Emotional Abuse.* Fleming H. Company, 1995.

Ketterman, Grace. *Verbal Abuse.* Servant Publications, 1993.

Kingsolver, Barbara. *The Poisonwood Bible.* Harper Perennial, 1999.

Lamb, Wally. *She's Come Undone.* Regan Books, 1992.

Surshen, Karin L. *Domestic Violence.* Greenhaven Press, 1996.

Weldon, Michele. *I Closed My Eyes: Revelations of A Battered Woman.* Hazelden Publishing, 1999.

ARE YOU REALLY OR SURREALLY IN LOVE?

Dryden, Carolina. *Being Married, Doing Gender: Critical Analysis of Gender Relationships in Marriage.* Routledge, 1999.

Gray, John. *Men Are from Mars, Women Are from Venus.* Harper Collins, 1992.

Hayes, Jody. *Smart Love: Changing Painful Patterns, Choosing Healthy Relationships.* Putnam Publishing Group, 1989.

Hendrix, Harville. *Getting the Love You Want: A Guide for Couples*. Harper Perennial, 1990.

Lerner, Harriet Goldhor. *The Dance of Intimacy: A Woman's Guide to Courageous Acts of Change in Key Relationships*. Harper and Row, 1989.

Norwood, Robin. *Women Who Love Too Much: When You Keep Wishing and Hoping He'll Change*. Simon & Schuster, 1990.

Peabody, Susan. *Addiction to Love: Overcoming Obsession and Dependency in Relationships*. Ton Ipead Press, 1994.

Porterfield, Kay Marie. *Violent Voices: Twelve Steps to Freedom from Emotional Abuse*. Health Communications, Inc., 1989.

Spezzano, Chuck. *If It Hurts, It Isn't Love*. Marlowe & Co., 1996.

Townsend, John Marshall. *What Women Want—What Men Want: Why the Sexes Still See Love and Commitment So Differently*. Oxford University Press, 1998.

Fiorenza, Elisabeth Schussler, and M. Shawn Copeland, eds. *Violence against Women— Concilium*. Orbis Books, 1994.

Weldon, Michelle. *I Closed My Eyes: Revelations of a Battered Woman*. Hazelden Publishing, 1999.

TAKE CHARGE TO LOVE, HONOR, AND CHERISH THYSELF

Awiakta, Marilou. *Seeking the Corn Mother's Wisdom*. Fulcrum Publishing, 1993.

Blaker, Karen, Born to Please. Little Brown & Co., 1986.

Boston Women's Health Collective. *Our Bodies, Ourselves.* Touchstone, 1998.

Bradshaw, John. *Creating Love.* Bantam Books, 1992.

Brown, William D. *Welcome Stress! It Can Help You Be Your Best.* Hazelden Information & Educational Services, 1983.

Covey, Stephen R. *The Seven Habits of Highly Effective People.* Simon & Schuster, 1989.

De Rosis, Helen. *Women & Anxiety: A Step-by-Step Program for Managing Anxiety and Depression.* Delacorte Press, 1979.

Goleman, Daniel. *Emotional Intelligence.* Bantam Books, 1995.

Kaltreider, Nancy B. *Dilemmas of a Double Life: Women Balancing Careers and Relationships.* Jason Aronson Publishers, 1997.

Hansen Shaevitz, Marjorie. *The Confident Woman: How to Take Charge and Recharge Your Life.* Harmony Books, 1999.

Jack, Dana Crowley. *Silencing the Self: Women and Depression.* Harper Perennial, 1993.

Lamb, Wally. *I Know This Much Is True.* Simon & Schuster, 1993.

LaMott, Anne. *Traveling Mercies: Some Thoughts on Faith.* Pantheon Books, 1999.

O'Connor, Richard. *Undoing Depression: What Therapy Doesn't Teach You and Medication Can't Give You.* Little Brown & Co., 1997.

Oliver, Gary J., and H. Norman Wright. *Good Women Get Angry: A Woman's Guide to Handling Her Anger, Depression,*

Anxiety, and Stress. Servant Publications, 1995.

Orbach, Susie. *What's Really Going On Here?* Virago, 1994.

Worchester, Nancy, and Marianne Whatley. *Women's Health: Readings on Social, Economic and Political Issues*. Kendall/Hunt, 1994.

Anapol, Deborah. *Polyamory: The New Love without Limits*. Intinet Resource Center, 1997.

Brody, Steve, and Cathy Brody. *Renew Your Marriage at Midlife*. New York: G.P. Putnam's Sons, 1999.

Brooks, Gary. *Centerfold Syndrome: How Men Can Overcome Objectification and Achieve Intimacy with Women*. John Wiley & Sons, 1995.

Cane, William. *The Art of Hugging: The World-Famous Kissing Coach Offers Inspiration and Advice on Why, Where, and How to Hug*. Saint Martin's Griffin, 1996.

Dale, Paulette. *Did You Say Something Susan?: How Any Woman Can Gain Confidence with Assertive Communication*. Carol Publishing Group, 1999.

Diamond, Jed. *Looking for Love in All the Wrong Places: Overcoming Romantic and Sexual Addictions*. Putnam, 1988.

Faludi, Susan, and Warren Farrell. "Warren Farrell vs. Susan Faludi." <http://www.menweb.org/farrfalu.html>, 1999.

Firestone, Robert W., and Joyce Catlette. *Fear of Intimacy*. American Psychological Association, 2000.

Gray, Barbara. *Life's Instruction Book for Women*. Royal Printing, 1994.

Gray, John. *Men Are from Mars, Women Are from Venus*. Harper Collins, 1992.

Kalbfleisch, Pamela J., and Michael J. Cody, eds. *Gender, Power, and Communication in Human Relationships*. Lawrence Erlbaum Associates, 1995.

Mansfield, Joe. <http://www.helpformen.com>.

Ornish, Dean. *Love & Survival: The Scientific Basis for the Healing Power of Intimacy*. Harper Collins, 1998.

Owen-Towle, Tom, and Chris Hassett. *Friendship Chronicles: Letters between a Gay and a Straight Man*. Bald Eagle Mountain Press, 1994.

Reichman, Judith. *I'm Not in the Mood: What Every Woman Should Know about Improving Her Libido*. Morrow/Avon, 1998.

Tannen, Deborah. *Gender and Discourse*. First Ballentine Books, 1990.

Tannen, Deborah. *That's Not What I Meant!* First Ballentine Books, 1990.

Tannen, Deborah. *You Just Don't Understand*. First Ballentine Books, 1990.

Wolf, Sharyn. *How to Stay Lovers for Life*. Penguin Putnam, Inc., 1998.

Wood, Julia T. *Gendered Lives: Communication, Gender, and Culture*. Wadsworth Publishing, 1997.